THIS TIME IT'S PERSONAL

ANGEL PATHS TAROT

JAN SHEPHERD

CONTENTS

ACKNOWLEDGMENTS

Special and important thanks:

When you get to the point where a work like this is finished, and you look back across the journey you have just taken, there are always so many people to thank – so – it's that time again: these are the people who made this book happen.

All of the Healing Team and the subscribers to the erstwhile private area on Angel Paths - your interest and feedback drove me on, even when I felt much more inclined to lie down and have a nice rest; to each and all visitors to Angel Paths whose contributions make the site the place it is; to my animals who have, in their various ways, got in my way, cuddled me, patted me on the nose and generally told me it was time for tea; to Ellie – a more faithful, encouraging and generous editor/friend/supporter/thing-monster (private joke and no I am not explaining it unless she demands it) person you would not find anywhere else at all; Amanda Weibe, whose artistry and vision has once again made my images for me (check out the aura man – he's lovely); and finally, to each and every one of you who purchase and read this book.

I wish you well on your personal journeys, and trust that we will meet along the path, to sit down and share our experiences, our ups, our downs and our visions one with another. Light Bearers are the essence of hope. Never stop believing that each and every one of us can, and does, make a difference.

Thank you all. Each of you is precious.

Loadsa love

Jan Shepherd
October 2014

INTRODUCTION

When most people first come into contact with Tarot, it is usually through its predictive medium – they visit somebody for a reading, perhaps, and that psychic uses a deck. Even where Tarot appears in pop-culture – as in the Bond movie "Live and Let Die" - the cards are featured as a means of seeing into the future.

Yet for me, this capacity to foretell events is a side effect of Tarot's central focus. I see Tarot as one of the essential tools in the process of self-discovery and development. Each card presents us with a facet of human experience – and often accompanies this with a viable method of meeting that event in a fashion that will yield the best result or outcome for us.

This book sets out to tease out the intricate personal lessons that we can glean from using Tarot as a teaching medium, rather than a mirror to the future. Here we will try to understand how to fine-tune our sensitivity to, and understanding of, the complex messages the cards offer us.

I often say to querents (a querent is the person asking for a reading) that Tarot can present us with a kind of "road-map" to life if we approach it in the right way – even when our contact comes from a predictive reading. When we decide to deliberately employ the Tarot in this fashion, we acquire a faithful and sometimes painfully truthful friend to guide us through each and every challenge life places in our path.

A Tarot deck comprises 78 cards – 22 of these are "Major Arcana" cards which represent prime archetypes and which should be regarded as very powerful influences. The remaining 66 cards are divided into Suits (much like a regular deck of cards). Each of these Suits corresponds to one of the Elements thought to make up material existence.

The structure of Tarot has a close correlation to the ancient system of belief known as the Quabbala. This glyph and its associated lore is derived from Hebrew origins. Whilst it is not my intent in this work to go deeply into Quabbala itself, it is useful to understand the existence of this connection. Quabbala has been described as the universal Filing System – and it certainly functions as such – everything has its appointed place and each link between one topic and another can be explored and examined in order to learn more about its function in life.

We will examine each card in sequence, seeking to explore the complex spiritual messages behind each, but always with an eye to furthering our developing intimate relationship with Self, and with Spirit – and when I say Spirit, I am referring to that scintillating fragment of perfection and truth with which each of us are equipped immediately prior to our very first incarnation. We will carry that fragment with us, life to life, attempting and striving to grow it from tiny glittering spark to dazzling torch carried by us – the completed Light Bearer. After all – that IS the point of all this, isn't it?

Essential components in this process are that we each learn to know and accept ourselves in our entirety - the brightest and the darkest of us, and all quicksilver shades between - and that we develop a set of ethics which is robust, well-rounded and eventually, an integral part of our every thought.

We are partners in the journey toward the Higher Self – therein will we discover the doorway which opens to reveal the ultimate

Truths of the Universe, and meet with the Gatekeeper who will welcome us home.

Methods of working with the material in this book

I am hoping that you will find the commentaries in this book inspiring, enjoyable, challenging and thought-provoking. There are many different ways in which you might choose to use them. I thought I might suggest a few ideas for you. Perhaps one (or some) of these ideas will appeal to you, or maybe you will want to devise a method unique to you. Either way, there is no "right" way of doing things.

You might decide to sign up for the Angel Paths Card of the Day email, or check the site and Facebook page each day to discover which card I have drawn to cover that period. You might choose to select a personal Card of the Day for yourself, and work with that.

Alternatively it might appeal to you much more to work your way through the deck in standard order. This has the advantage that you will not get repeating cards (unless you choose to go back to one yourself) and you will have considered each card in the deck in the light of daily life in just under three months. On the other hand, though, a single day's consideration of a specific set of influences is probably nowhere near sufficient.

Learning to live your life in accordance with the "rules" set out in a Tarot deck is both challenging and revealing. The underpinning gnosis of Tarot will also be found in religious credo and some philosophical trains of thought. Much of it will feel familiar from the outset. You will probably have already incorporated some ideas into your approach to life. But hopefully by working with this book you will gain a greater understanding of how everything "hangs together" – how each concept grows from the ones around it, coloured and tempered by its neighbours.

The practice of meditation can help to release new thoughts. If you have never tried to meditate perhaps now is a good time to start. I strongly recommend the book "Moon Over Water" by Jessica MacBeth as a really accessible and helpful guide to meditation. If you learn to slip easily into a meditative state, it can introduce a whole new dimension to life, whether you are studying the Tarot or simply trying to recharge in a demanding environment.

Perhaps even more important to developing a real working insight into living your life in line with Tarot is the application of the influence of a particular card to the events and circumstances you encounter in an ordinary day – bringing the power of the Emperor to a pitch at work, the insight of the Priestess to a contentious meeting, the innate wisdom and tenderness of the Empress to negotiations with a wilful or disobedient youngster – these can deepen your own richness of experience, and encourage you to bring the best of yourself to any situation.

Each of these 78 cards reflects back to us a different take on life itself, a facet of human experience which we will meet at some point on our journey. A strong recognition of each facet's nuance and variation equips us efficiently to approach life from a position of harmony with spirit, and light. In this way, we offer all that we can to this race of ours.

At the end of the book you will discover two separate exercises. Each is a form of protection, and I recommend that you experiment with both of them. The aura exercise strengthens the auric field, and seals it, guarding you from unwanted external intrusions. The Lesser Banishing Ritual cleanses the area it covers, expelling negativity and creating a "clean" safe space, which remains shielded for some hours. Over time, both of these exercises build in depth and potency through repetition. They each also familiarise you with your own personal space – a real tool in this busy and often intrusive world of hours. I hope I have given you some good ideas for making use of this book. Enjoy!

THE MAJOR ARCANA

THE FOOL

Thoth Tarot - The Fool

Have you ever considered what it is like to live without fear? To feel wholly in harmony with life? To feel that each day brings only happy goodness into your life? Many people would say that this is an impossible state within which to exist. Yet in some respects it is one of our end goals in our spiritual quest.

When we are able to surrender fear and self-doubt, when we can develop the ability to trust in life and in ourselves, we set a vital part of our inner being free to create whatever we need.

Fear stops us from trying to meet those challenges we feel threatened by. It stops us from taking vital steps toward our own independence. When we are frozen by fear, we find it impossible to move out of our inertia, and to do the things which would lay our anxieties to rest.

When I feel afraid, there are two phrases which I repeat like mantras... "there is no courage without fear", and "feel the fear and do it anyway". Somehow the combination of the two seems to keep me moving forward even though I'm not sure quite what will happen next.

The Fool is the epitome of fearlessness. It is not that he does not perceive the hazards before him, as some commentators would have you think. It is that he knows that his own resilience and his trust in the gods will keep him safe.

He believes that nothing happens for no reason, and that all problems are, in truth, challenges awaiting his resolution. Of course, this is easy to say, and hard to apply. But we can try. We can choose to overcome obstacles with a positive heart and a deep-seated trust both in ourselves, and in the energies which drive us.

When we decide that we are going to attempt to live this way, there is one vital ingredient that we must never leave out. We must always, without fail, acknowledge the fact that we have faced and conquered a fear. We often do not do this... rather, we think we were wrong to have the fear in the first place. There must be reward and acceptance every single time we conquer a fear. That way we feel more prepared to tackle the next one.

THE MAGUS

Thoth Tarot - The Magus

This card is, quite simply, about the power of Will. A disbelief in our own willpower is one of the great malaises of mankind. Too often, we believe we cannot make a difference. Too often, we believe we cannot achieve the summit of success and happiness we yearn for. Too often, we believe that we are ineffectual against the forces around us.

Yet this ignores one perfectly obvious factor. What we are, what we do, what we dream, the fact that we exist at all, is a major miracle which attests to our own power. Think of the mighty achievements (or damnations, depending on your point of view) of mankind. Look at what our race has already accomplished. Examine the feats of mighty engineering that have created our world. Consider the miracles of modern science. Contemplate what our race is capable of doing.

And, instead of creating external heroes, realise that every single one of our achievements has come from one single person's initial concept. A single person. Not a superman or woman, but a person... just like you and me.

Every great leap forward of technology, every medical advance, every scientific realisation, has come from one person's mind. Right at the very beginning, before the pyramids were built, before we discovered penicillin, before we harnessed the life in the wind and the sea for power, somebody thought of the idea.

Before organisations like Greenpeace, the World Wildlife Fund, UNICEF grew up... one person thought they would be a good idea. Just one ordinary person – a person like you or me. A person with faults, flaws, failings, doubts, uncertainties, just like you and me. A person with the vision, determination and self-belief to think that they COULD make a difference.

They were all just ordinary folk who had the courage to trust themselves and the force of life. They were people brave enough to risk the pain of disappointment weighed against the sweet ecstasy of success.

You are a person. You can do anything. You are your own Magus of Power; your own dream weaver; your own sculptor of life. What you do, what you think, what you Will shapes what comes next. Make every act an act of creation – a building block toward the future you want to live. You make a difference.

THE PRIESTESS

Thoth Tarot - The Priestess

This card is surrounded by an aura of mystery which can sometimes make it quite difficult to get to grips with – yet it is that very air of mystery which reveals the largest part of its inner gnosis.

Most people who have studied Tarot would agree that one of the really hard things about getting the hang of accurate reading is learning how to simply allow the intuition to function. When one card can have countless nuances of interpretative meaning, it is difficult to figure out which aspect applies at the time of reading. Until the reader achieves the knack of making contact with their intuition, they will tend to limit themselves to a fairly restricted choice of explanation.

However once they manage to cross the barrier which exists between the conscious and the subconscious mind they will find their ability to analyse a reading will expand. It's the barrier-crossing that causes the problem – and also which lends so much mystery to the Priestess card, for a deep understanding of this card lies beyond that barrier.

It is a peculiarity of our modern times that we have tended to lay down certain of the acute senses that our ancestors so sharply honed. Psychism and intuition have been two of the most severe casualties in our gallop toward science and proof. Whilst there is great benefit to be had from the first of these, and a pressing need for the second, they are not the only things that count in life. Our ability to reach beyond the factoid barrier, and into our instinctual senses, has slipped through our fingers to an alarming extent.

We actively disconnect children from their imagination with an almost brutal disregard for the consequences. Fairies must stop living in fuchsias at just about the same time that we learn to name them, and the shadows we see on the edge of reality are just bad dreams that we mustn't disturb our parents by talking about. The heightened perception and acceptance of a comprehensive reality is ripped away from us and replaced with a monotone world in no time at all. And then we have the sheer frustration, in later life, of struggling to regain what we had as a colourful and inherent part of our nature when we first came into the world.

Meditation is one way of releasing your inherent psychic sense. People tend to shy away from practices like this – they don't have time, or they can't get the hang of it. But giving yourself a little time in each day to simply let your mind drift is not such a bad thing. And it will surely benefit you to separate yourself from the hurly burly bustle for just a few still moments and listen to what is going on deep within you. (Moon Over Water by Jessica Williams MacBeth is my go to reference for meditation). Try it for a little while... you'll be surprised what you discover that you didn't know you knew.

THE EMPRESS

Thoth Tarot - The Empress

This card represents the goddess both within and beyond us. She is the embodiment of perfect, enduring, unconditional love. The whole concept of pure mother love flows from this card as a direct representation of the essence of the Goddess.

One thing I have always been saddened by in monotheistic faiths is the way that the Divine Female is submerged beneath the weight of patriarchy. The loss of the female has denied us all something blessed – the knowledge of an intimate contact with whatever we define as the archetypal female force. As you probably know, I ascribe to the idea that there are many 'godforces', some male in nature, some female and some genderless. And my personal interaction with these forces has given me understanding, great comfort and, hopefully, a little wisdom.

I think it is terribly sad that our society tends to ignore one or more of them. A cuddle from that energy source that I call Goddess is mighty. In difficult periods She offers me reserves of strength and energy I did not know I was capable of. When I suffer, she soothes. When I am confused, she clarifies.

Whether these feelings come from outside me, or from some undiscovered realm within, I have no real idea. I choose, to an extent, to externalise my contact with the Divine Female – but I do also absorb and learn from that energy source.

There is a visualisation I came across once which was intended to lead you to your inner Goddess. For those of you who want to experiment, here is an abbreviated version of it.

Choose a safe space, where you can be quiet. Raise your protections in your usual way. Now imagine that you are climbing down a stone spiral staircase. When you come to the bottom of the staircase, you see that a narrow tunnel leads away. Light glows on the rock walls from the further end of the tunnel. You feel warm and excited as you walk slowly along it. The light grows brighter. Then as you turn a corner you find yourself stepping into a small natural cavern. A trickle of water makes a waterfall across the far side of the room. In the middle of the room is a throne heaped with cushions and draped with velvet. Upon this throne sits your representation of the Goddess. Spend some time with her, and take note of the details you see. When you want to leave, thank her for her attention, return down the corridor and climb the stairs back into your everyday life. Write down everything you remember.

THE EMPEROR

Thoth Tarot - The Emperor

One of the most revealing things you can do when studying the Emperor (especially if you use a Thoth deck) is to place his card alongside the Empress card. You will notice that light is shed upon the throned Emperor from two directions... one from above and slightly to the right of his body (active, dominant side) and the other from the Empress seated upon her throne beside him.

The Empress provides the stream of steady, enduring, unconditional, love that a man of his status needs to keep his feet on the ground, and allow him the room to lead from a position of strength, trusting always that he has constant support. The light from above is that of the gods or the Universe, driving him toward his purpose.

The Emperor, at his highest level, is the shepherd and ruler of us all. He is a powerful and decisive being upon whom we rely for guidance, and assistance in achieving our goals. But who leads the leader?

The unity between the Empress and the Emperor is not only an external influence. We all have active, dynamic sides to our personalities as well as the more passive, nurturing, ongoing aspect which is embodied by the Empress.

To extend this understanding of our archetypal make-up to its greatest extent we need also to introduce the effects of the High Priestess and the Magus – also aspects of ourselves. Each of us has these threads of humanity within us to one extent or another – they create the four elements within. The Magus is of Air, the High Priestess is of Water, the Empress is of Earth and the Emperor is of Fire. These four, synthesised correctly, produce the Hierophant who in turn guides us toward the self love which is the highest concept of the Lovers card and finally to the triumph inherent in the Chariot. These cards, which begin with the Fool, produce the inner part of our journey towards our gods.

There are three hepdomads (a group of seven) within the Major Arcana, all of which may be prefaced by the Fool. Each describes a stage in human spiritual expansion – this first here, comprising the Magus to the Chariot encapsulates internal development; the second, from Adjustment to Art, teach us how to bridge the vast gap between personal awareness and the natural, all powerful forces of the

Universe; and the third, outlined by those cards from the Devil to the Universe, enable us to step into the flow of Universal consciousness, as we attempt to express our understanding into daily life.

Within the Emperor, we find our personal power, our knowledge of 'rightness', and our ability to forge forward. He is supported by the nourishment of the Empress, informed by the knowledge and skill of the Magus and guided by the intuition of the High Priestess... and he embarks upon his purpose with confidence and a sense of self reliance.

THE HIEROPHANT

Thoth Tarot - The Hierophant

Some commentators maintain that the Hierophant is about tradition and maintaining the status quo. This is a misunderstanding of the occult aspect of the card. In fact part of the inner lore of the Hierophant is about entering into a tradition, rather than to do with keeping things the way they are for no good reason.

It is a specific type of tradition to which the card refers – a magickal order for example... or an established religion. The defining factor here is that these deal with beliefs and philosophies which have developed into a credo over a period of time (and possibly deteriorated into dogma).

At the head of such orders and religions we find the High Priest – spiritual leader, possibly blessed by Divine Right. This person makes a bridge of themselves between the gods and mankind. S/he is mediator, interpreter, mentor and teacher.

The original hierophant presided over the Eleusian Mysteries, The word itself breaks down to hiero- holy and the –phant part means 'to reveal' or 'to show'. It is the function of the Hierophant to reveal the Mysteries to the solemn seeker.

Much of spiritual and occult development is based on the student's ability to see ordinary things in a different light. As discussed in the commentary about the Universe in this section, life tends to unwind in spirals. The same is true of occult development. It generally cycles through familiar territory, on a gradually widening arc.

Only when we are ready to make certain important realisations will we find ourselves equipped with the ability and skill to make them. Our progression might be seen as developing as a series of arcs. Each arc gives us an additional or greater insight on a specific area of understanding, the next always built and dependent upon the one preceding it. In this fashion we build the touchstone of our comprehensive of spiritual development. It is in gathering the necessary knowledge that we travel across developmental plateaus. When we finally reach the dizzyingly high cliff at the far side hopefully we shall have learned enough to allow us to scamper up the cliff-face without pause.

THE LOVERS

Thoth Tarot - The Lovers

Have you ever wondered why you embarked on this spiritual journey of yours? I have not met many people who feel they definitely know the answer to that question. We quest blindly, knowing that there is some immutable truth we are seeking – some revelation that will make sense of everything. Along the way we learn a new approach to life, and we gain many skills we had not expected... but still the yearning remains.

In almost all religious beliefs, there is reference to a 'joining with' the Highest Force. This is said to happen sometimes on death, and at others, after a vast amount of self-perfecting. Also, in most religions, the Higher Force, whatever its name, consists of pure love. When we join we shall become pure love ourselves. We will be filled to the brim with joy, lit from within by love, untroubled and tranquil.

The very imagining of being in that state can make your heart lurch can't it? There's something deep inside that remembers the blissful security of that experience. A memory perhaps, of some other, safer time.

Every now and again, as you follow your path, something will happen that fills up your heart with radiance. And for that second, everything is right with the world. Anything can trigger this attunement, if it feeds your soul and spirit – beautiful scenery, a child's smile, the wind in the willow tree.

I think this is one reason we place so much focus on intimate relationships. They give us greater opportunities to touch our souls. You know what it's like when you fall in love – the rush of passion and desire, the appreciation of beauty in another, the intense attention focussed upon the beloved. We come alive.

Unfortunately, as the saying goes, we have to kiss a lot of frogs before we find the handsome Prince (or beautiful Princess). I think we would save ourselves a lot of heartache if we lived in the belief that there is no point in kissing the toad just in case s/he is "The One". Far better we wait until we meet somebody who stirs our soul and sets light to our spirit before we give ourselves up as unconditionally as love demands we do.

We cannot make ourselves fall in love. Love comes from Universal

Energy. It inrushes when the right conditions prevail. It does not dribble in by accident because we think it should. Yet often we hurt ourselves in our search for love, getting into situations that we know from the outset will not suit us. One thing that helps us to learn that we can receive inrushes of love from the Universe is to practise the open breathing technique I mentioned in the working with section under the 6 of Cups. You will find this on the Angel Paths website, or in the book The Angel Paths Guide To The Tarot 2nd Edition. Try this often. You will be surprised at how it can lift your mood, ease your worries and help you to feel confident to live life to the full.

THE CHARIOT

Thoth Tarot - The Chariot

In the context of this book, where the focus is using the deck as a directive tool as mentioned in the introduction, the Chariot is a very important card. It indicates a centre point of stillness and self-reliance that allows the Will to unfold without hinder or obstacle. However it takes a great deal of practise to maintain that state of mind. Mundane things, or imaginal fears, can often shake us from our centre points. And each time this happens our Will (which is always functioning to one extent or another) can lurch out of control.

It is important, therefore, to practise entering your centre point, and learning how to rest safely within it whilst living your every day life. To achieve this position will give you a sense of well-being and strength. You can see in the illustration of this card, that the charioteer holds a rapidly spinning vortex. Crowley (the designer of this deck) says that the spinning orb represents the Holy Grail. In no way does the rider of the chariot appear connected with the beasts which draw the vehicle forward. He controls their direction and speed purely by the power of his own Will.

When the Will flows in a continuous surge at the desired end result, you will find yourself effortlessly moving toward your goals. There will be no doubt, no stumbling block, no delay. No frustrating hold-ups or collisions. The Chariot and its driver teach us that when we rest easy within ourselves, we will be victorious.

You may well already know where the centre of yourself is. But if you have not yet discovered it, you are missing a real treat, and giving yourself a hard time when it comes to applying what you are learning here. So it would be as well to consider exactly where and what this magickal place is.

First and foremost, the centre is a state of mind. But it can be quite helpful to imagine a place in which to experience that state of mind. When we rest in the centre, we do not think. We simply are. It is a balanced, restful, all-knowing awareness. We have an uncluttered view of ourselves. We are appreciative of the strengths within us and we do not dwell on the darker areas. We are at one with ourselves. Utterly contented. In order to achieve this blissful state, you could try something along the lines suggested below.

The place I keep my centre varies depending on my state of mind when I enter it. I might be sitting against a dry-stone wall up on the moors, with the wind in my hair, able to see forever. Or on a crag overlooking the incoming ocean, once again with the wind in my hair ;-) Or in a walled garden filled with fragrant flowers. You can use any scene that you feel fills you up and opens your soul.

When you get to wherever you decide to put your centre, walk inside, sit yourself down and begin to create every last little detail of the place. Imagine the creases and folds in the petals of flowers, the serrated edge of a leaf, the way the light shifts and changes as you make everything more real. If any stray everyday thoughts enter your mind push them aside and return to the minute creation of a place of beauty which you will come to call your centre.

You will probably need a few sessions of creation before you slide inside the state of mind.

If my description of this experience is not too clear, don't worry... when it happens you will know it has. And once you have achieved the feeling, store it away for future reference. And keep practising. The more you manage to live your life from the centre of your being, the easier it will become.

ADJUSTMENT

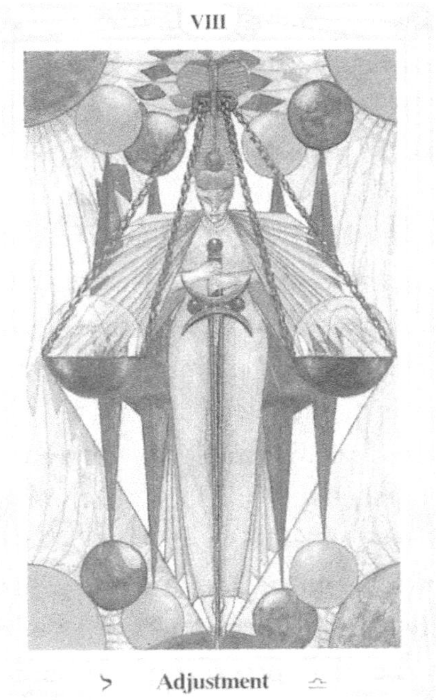

Thoth Tarot - Adjustment

For me Adjustment has always marked a point of pivot – the present we now exist within, with past and future stretching out before and behind. It marks the one and only thing upon which we can act – the moment. Previous actions and choices are cast, and unchanging. Once done, they cannot be undone. All we can learn to do is accept, acknowledge and let go.

But this moment – this very moment here, in which you read these words – this gives you the greatest opportunity of your life - the opportunity to shape your mutable future; the chance to establish something new and hopeful and happy in coming days; the possibility to take a life-changing decision, the consequence of which will alter the direction of your journey.

Our experience of the 'now' is quite poorly developed. Too often we think about past events, and worry about the future. Both really are a waste of time. When we dwell upon past events, we stop shaping our futures – or worse still, we shape our futures to look precisely the same as our past. And if we are anxious about what the future holds then we flood coming days with worry and concern.

Once we can get the knack of regarding every moment as golden with promise – a priceless gift from life itself – we can begin the process of dreaming our future. The more clearly we can see our current situation as the result of past events the more we begin to want to engage with the creation of a worthwhile and happy future.

So whenever this card comes up, I like to practise "being in the moment". For me this moment looks like this:

I am sitting at my desk in front of the computer, typing. My shoulders ache a bit. If I glance up I can look out through the window into the garden. I can see the light on the leaves of the rhododendron beyond the window. Distantly I can hear cars passing by. My phone is ringing ;-) And here I am in another moment – because I cannot type quickly enough to be able to tell you everything about that other moment...

This work-out of the senses will teach you a great deal about how complex and varied are the streams of information with which you are informed at all times. The more you use it, the more acute it will become. Learning to really listen to each of your senses in a moment-by-moment fashion is remarkably helpful in terms of positioning yourself in your life. Naturally, it is not something we can engage in continuously – but developing a greater level of awareness in this area by applying ourselves for very short bursts of attention increases our overall recognition of this astounding process.

THE HERMIT

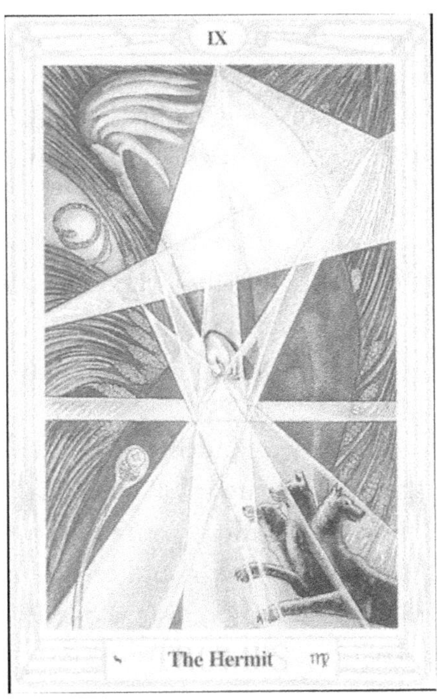

Thoth Tarot - The Hermit

Most versions of the Hermit show a man carrying a lantern. This card is, first and foremost, about the journey we take toward ourselves. The lantern is our own inner light – the light that we often forget whilst surviving the trials and tribulations of life.

We disregard the fact that we are, in fact, sheaths of flesh, which wraps and protects an inner flaming spark of pure essential spirit. And in losing sight of this, we lose one of the most precious experiences a human can have. We begin to live our lives outside in, instead of inside out.

The reason so many of us embark on this spiritual journey is because we feel a yearning to touch the very core of ourselves – to know...once and for all... what we really are all about. We need to develop an essential knowledge of ourselves, our purpose, our mission, our talents and skills. And we shall only do this when we accept ourselves in entirety.

The Hermit is about that inner soul journey. And he reveals an important wisdom to us simply by showing us the image on the card. We tend to believe that our inner light is somewhere buried deep within us... something hidden within the furthest reaches of our spirits.

But it isn't. The Hermit carries the light before him all the way along the journey. It is the light which shows him where he is going. The deepest reaches of our spirit are here, with us, at all times. We just need to know how to touch them, and to draw them into everyday awareness.

We often overcomplicate the process of spiritual development, by estranging it from the routine pattern of daily life. And yet if we study those patterns with an open mind, we may recognise that we are surrounded by magick and mystery in our every moment. The things we take for granted, and scarcely register consciously, are often the very building blocks of realisation and growth.

FORTUNE

Thoth Tarot - Fortune

Embedded deep within the card Fortune is the secret of knowing our own Life Goals. Once upon the spiritual path it is not long before the journeyer begins to ask "What's it all for? What am I meant to be doing?" The belief that there is a point to life is inherent to the search for the vast 'itness' of spirituality. We may come to believe that we do not live just one life... or that once we move on from this life there is something infinitely more rewarding waiting on the other side. We assess thoughts and ideas about Karma, trying to understand how our actions affect the things that manifest in our lives. It is fair to say that we are questing... and this raises many questions.

One of the most personal questions to which we shall ever seek the answer is "Where do I fit in the fullness of life?" This can reach the proportions of yearning if we find it difficult to form an answer – and we often do.

It is this area that the Wheel of Fortune helps us to uncover. Return often to quiet meditation of this card, whilst holding the question in mind. Let yourself think over the things you love to do, the activities that most reward you, the interests you return to again and again. When you can achieve an overview of all these areas, you will see a certain coherence. Somewhere in there is your Life Goal.

Some people believe that, before returning to 'the redness of life', we pause and take stock of what we have learned in preceding lives. Then we decide what it is we need to experience or learn this time around. Once we have set our goals, we select an environment in which we may achieve our aspirations and learn our lessons.

Opponents of this view often counter it by saying "But who would choose to experience terrible events which scar them for life?" The answer to that question would probably be "In order that the rounded spirit can empathise, it must enter into dark events, as well as happy ones".

Another perspective on the birth environment is that it comes as a direct check and balance against the individual's Karmic development. In this case, if a person has sinned against another at some time in their past, they will be placed in a circumstance which teaches them not to deal so unkindly with others again.

I don't know which of these viewpoints is true – though I ascribe to the first one. I prefer to believe that we select certain learning experiences in order to grow our spirits. However perhaps each viewpoint is true to a certain extent – maybe events are imposed on a younger spirit and selected by a more experienced one.

Either way – the search for the Life Goal, and your subsequent attempts to fulfil that goal, are part of your driving force in search for spiritual development, so it's as well to give the subject some thought.

LUST

Thoth Tarot - Lust

In the section on working with the Lust card I gave you an exercise to try in order to help you achieve Right Attention. You might like to go back to it now. Right Attention is an attitude of mind that we would all do well to work on occasionally. It allows us to truly engage our senses within the immediate moment. It is quite amazing how much information and input we filter out during the course of daily life.

As I concentrate now in putting these words onto the screen I am ignoring the sound of cars passing by, the hum of my computer, the sound of a scroll wheel on the other side of the room. Whilst each of these things is obvious if I listen for them, I blot them out so that I can concentrate.

When engaged in certain tasks it is useful to have this ability – but it is an indiscriminate skill. When we focus on one particular topic or activity to the exclusion of all others we can miss important clues that life is trying to give to us. The practice of Right Attention as a regular part of our day, gives us more opportunities to hear what the Universe is saying to us – and also the opportunity to glory in the moment, an activity which definitely does not receive the attention it deserves.

The threads which weave the tapestry of life are infinitely varied and convoluted. Life is such an intricate process that it is easy to lose sight of the sheer wonder to which we are witness on a daily basis. The Lust card is, more than anything else, about allowing our inner passion the room to burn freely with a bright light that clarifies all around it.

If we live life feeling it is a burden, we deny ourselves some wonderful experiences. This is even more true when we are passing through hard times, when events conspire to hurt us, and we feel trust is in short supply. The Lust card gives us the strength to carry on. It gives us the ability to find beauty despite any pain we may feel. It gives us the grace to see that we are blessed.

THE HANGED MAN

Thoth Tarot - The Hanged Man

Above all, the Hanged Man is about acceptance and surrender. There are times in every life when there is, quite simply, nothing we can do save trust. When we are faced with this type of situation it is probably one of the most difficult and demanding for us to learn from.

By nature we expect to be able to effect a change upon our environment. Even when we accept that we are helpless we torture ourselves with "what ifs" and "if onlys". We can go to the lengths of thoroughly beating ourselves up, rather than accept that certain experiences are wholly unavoidable in life.

And it is true that the Gods are unwilling to do that for us, which we are perfectly able to do for ourselves. So in many cases, effort and travail are necessary in order to achieve our goals.

However, on the spiritual path, there will come a moment of perfect inevitability. When examined through the lens of hindsight we will recognise that the forces and events which surround us have inexorably led us to a point where there is nothing left to do but accept and surrender.

We can fight as much as we like. We can wriggle like hooked fish, attempting to escape the line. We can thrash and flail as much as we want... but whatever we do we must, in the end, become the Hanged Man.

Poised between the mundane and the divine we are forced to stop, and consider – to capitulate to the Will of the forces of life. And when we can finally manage to do that... we will probably be on the receiving end of the greatest realisations, revelations and gifts we have ever imagined.

Life is a wise, if brutal, teacher at times. Of course, we make this process more difficult for ourselves by learning much more effectively from our pain than we ever do our pleasure. But either way, when the lesson becomes imperative, we will learn it, one way or another. How much easier it is to become the Hanged Man for a time, welcoming in even the most uncomfortable of realisations.

DEATH

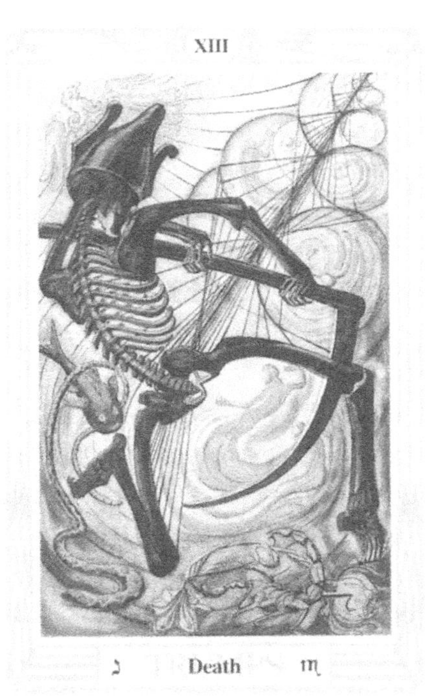

Thoth Tarot - Death

I wonder if you have ever pondered the process of esoteric initiation? To a great many people this can mean being involved in a shadowy ritual in a darkened room with some people (possibly cowled and robed) which makes you a member of a secret society ;-).

Whilst I have no doubt such ceremonies take place somewhere on the planet, this is not what initiation means. To initiate means to begin... in the esoteric sense we could apply it to the point at which you seriously committed yourself to a deliberate and lifelong study of the Mysteries – whichever aspect appeals to you. It is the intent and commitment which matter, rather than any particular ceremony which surrounds that act – though it is true that being initiated by a person further along the spiritual path than yourself can provide a considerable "leg-up" in terms of progress. The Neophyte gains a gift of the Master's power in that situation.

Inherent to the concept of initiation is the idea that you will study, gathering to you a body of information around your chosen subject. We're fortunate (or spoiled) these days compared to our ancestors. There is a wealth of knowledge available right now at your local bookshop. Less than a century ago we could not have obtained many informed writings by explorers of the hidden realms. But today there are, quite literally, thousands of volumes available – not all of them good, and not all of them to be taken on face value. Luckily amid the dross are some real gems which assist you in the process of opening your mind to the unknown.

Many people feel that they do need a hands-on teacher – but this is becoming less and less the case I suspect. Whilst to be taught by a Master is a great honour, reserved for the very select and fortunate few, the lack of a teacher will not necessarily stop you from making good progress along your chosen path.

With increasingly easy communication it becomes simpler to gain knowledge from a variety of learned people – through websites such as Angel Paths, for instance, whose communities are regularly visited by a range of people – from total beginners, right the way through to highly experienced light-workers. These days we can learn from a multiplicity of sources, each of which contributes some more to the whole of our knowledge.

Why have I chosen to discuss initiation when the Death card comes up? Because at the centre of this card is the concept that again and again we make commitments and choices which change our lives irrevocably. And when we do we experience a Death in miniature. When we decide to commit to another person, for instance, we experience the death of our life as a single person. When we make career changes, we experiences the death of ourselves as, say, stock broker in order to become a brain surgeon. And when we commit to a study of the Mysteries, we experience the death of ourselves as we previously were.

In records of initiation ceremonies, the probationer was often put through a series of trials – many of which simulated death, to symbolise that when we walk the esoteric path, we surrender that which came before. We will never be the same. Life has changed beyond measure. We are reborn into a spiritual exploration which will continue to alter our perspective for the rest of our lives. In the normal course of spiritual development, there are many initiations as our understanding and insight expand – some relatively minor "light-bulb" moments, and others seed changes at the very core of us. This is how we learn to unfold the spiritual being within ourselves.

ART

Thoth Tarot - Art

Hopefully we already recognise the qualities that Art (or Temperance in traditional decks) teaches us of patience, of living from the centre of our beings, of allowing life to flow through and around us. There is a remarkable sense of relaxation when we achieve this willingness to release ourselves to drift with the currents of life. Moreover this ability often carries us in unexpected directions, informing and teaching us along the way. Naturally, it requires a certain self-trust and confidence – and perhaps also the innocence of the Fool.

But here I want to talk with you about why Temperance had its name changed to Art. The Art referred to here is the High Magickal Art of achieving what is known as The Great Work. In most traditions this concept exists as the major reason for spiritual growth and striving, no matter what the tradition calls it.

The Great Work is the perfection of Self – the living embodiment of highest spiritual principles, walking around in a body on the face of the planet. This is the perfected being, who has broken the hold of Karma – broken free of the Wheel of Life. As you can imagine, these are relatively rare beings, who have been aeons in the completing. In modern parlance, ordinary people tend to refer to such beings as "angels", "saviours" and so on. In fact, they are those remarkable individuals who can live from the centre of Spirit, rather than being rooted into mundane life.

If you examine that eternal question "What's it all about?" in the end you will come to the conclusion that you want to create a happy life for yourself, living within a set of ethics you are contented with, making enough money to feed yourself, and being surrounded by love. And then you want to proceed to live a fulfilling joyous life, in which you not only revel in what you have, but pursue actions for others which indicate your gratitude for your good fortune. That is a way of journeying toward the completion of The Great Work – to live in harmony with life and people, and give of yourself good things to the Universe, in the sure knowledge that you will receive good things in return.

If you take this state one stage further, and say that you want to do this with knowledge, wisdom and the conscious awareness of a spiritual quest, you have the depth of understanding that allows you experiential contact with the Universe.

If you examine the perfect balance inherent in this card you will see that all things are reflected, one to the other. All aspects of life are balanced evenly. Each aspect receives the required attention in the right measure at the right time. The quicksilver mind is challenged, the material needs are fully met, the heart is still and full, and the spirit soars in freedom. It is in this state that we finally achieve the unlimited contact with the Universe that we seek.

It is a state which must be created and re-created a hundred times a day – but it is a blissful state, which brings great clarity, liberty and grace when we can begin to achieve it. So, aim to be balanced. Aim to pay right attention to each thing in your life. And open yourself to the power of the Universe.

THE DEVIL

Thoth Tarot - The Devil

Have you ever spent time analysing what the root causes of aspects of evil are? It can be an interesting exercise, because almost every instance of mankind's evil is rooted in his/her animal nature. The driving forces which lead us to commit acts of evil (and we are all capable of them) are mostly instinctual. Even calculated acts of evil generally can be tracked back to instinct – though usually through a far more circuitous route...

What is even more interesting is to attempt to analyse acts of pure evil by the multitude of other animals with whom we share our planet. Acts of evil committed by animals are very few and far between. And noticeably those animals we do generally accept have a vicious streak (like domestic cats for example) have had close contact with humans over centuries.

As I said in the "Working with" series it is well worth exploring your own instinctual needs and acknowledging them – this way you can identify problematic areas, robbing them of their power to drive you subconsciously to commit acts that you will later regret.

Of course, one of the really tough things about admitting to your own darkness is that it is liable to make you feel quite uncomfortable... none of us like to think of ourselves as capable of committing acts of pure evil. Yet if we are to truly explore ourselves one of the things we must come to terms with is our own shadow self. And more than that, we must learn to accept it in a non-judgemental and caring fashion. Only by identifying our tendency to, for instance, lash out, run from fear of pain or threat, ill wish others, suffer from envy, etc etc, can we bring our lesser feelings under our conscious control. And it really does not help if, during this process, we give ourselves a hard time for the aspects of self that we dislike, or feel ashamed of.

We often avoid scrutinising our flaws. Yet there is enormous strength in knowing what you are really capable of. The darker sides of our personalities are motivated by deep passions, and compelling urges, which we cannot healthily eradicate from our beings. Therefore we must learn to not only identify, but also to own our personal lurking depths, attempting to adapt these until they appear more reasonable to us.

Interestingly, when we do embark on this search for our shadow self, we often make some revealing and important discoveries... the woman who never appears to lose her temper because it isn't 'nice', suddenly trips across a well of anger that she has been repressing all her life – and when she vents that anger, she realises that she has been damming a stream of vital energy and a method of expressing her own power that she needs, and desires.

The man who has been insecure in his status since puberty discovers his inhibitions about fantasising sexually, and in ridding himself of these releases a stream of sexual energy which makes him happy with his manhood, which introduces a positive and affirming strength into all areas of his life.

The possible examples could go on and on... but the major point here is that, as composite beings – half god/dess, half animal, we cannot afford to ignore nor deny our instincts. These are fundamental to our existence and survival. If they were not there, we probably would not be either. But we need to get to know them thoroughly... and to examine the consequences of denying or repressing them on our personalities. If those consequences are compelling enough, we will find it easy to begin to release our inner animals and allow them room to breathe. And in so doing we shall reduce the likelihood of doing evil – whether this be to ourselves or somebody else.

THE TOWER

Thoth Tarot - The Tower

This Major Arcanum tends to be one of the 'unpopular' cards because of its habit of presaging disruptive or frightening events over which the querent has little control. Whilst this meaning is perfectly valid in certain circumstances, it is only one aspect of the influence of the Tower.

I often associate the phrase "breakthrough or breakdown" with this card. It sums up the potential of the Tower. Often, even though we can see a particular course of action will benefit us enormously, we hesitate, hanging on to the familiar, rather than taking the plunge into new territory.

If we hesitate for long enough, when the Tower is ruling the day we shall find ourselves flung into the mêlée whether or not we are ready. Sometimes it is necessary to adopt the attitude of the Fool in life – being willing to change, even though we cannot see what the end result may be.

At those heady moments when we simply trust to life, we often make great leaps of understanding. We recognise that some of life's working is a mystery, and that our interpretations of reality can sometimes be so far from the truth as to be laughably inaccurate. When we can be brave enough to give ourselves permission to get things wrong occasionally, we free off a well-spring of power which has previously been caught up in hiding our perceived inadequacies from the rest of the world.

We are then unafraid to jump from the topmost window of the Tower if we believe that we can achieve safe landing in the new region of our life which has been revealed to us. We become like explorers in a foreign land, uncovering the fresh and delightful with every turn of the path we follow.

This can be the 'upside' of the Tower, that we learn to respond to challenge through the eyes of the Fool, leaving fear and self-limitation behind.

The "downside" of the Tower emerges when we will not allow change to flow readily through our lives. When we are inert, unwilling to take risks with trust, we begin to stagnate. The natural state of the human soul is to ever strive toward the perfection of spirit, so that we eventually achieve alignment with the Universe. When we fight against this impulse we introduce the disruption and pain of the Tower's march toward enlightenment.

THE STAR

Thoth Tarot - The Star

This is a buoyant and joyful card, filled with a kind of irresponsibility born of total trust. When we can achieve complete and faithful trust in the beneficence of the highest powers in life, there comes this mighty realisation that we may be free of worry and clutter. So long as we tread the path of gods and goddesses, our destiny will unfold, unfettered and even.

As we have already seen, this card brings in remarkable periods of opportunity and good fortune. The reason this happens is because, sometimes by accident, we manage to align ourselves with the Universal flow that passes through and around us in every second of our lives. It may be that, for a brief few weeks, planetary alignments influence us so favourably that we move into a period of success and achievement. We need to try as hard as we can to take advantage of such periods.

But more than that, we need to learn how to activate these favourable energies at will. Lust (Strength) has much to tell us about how we can create the harmony required to achieve this sense of at-oneness and equilibrium. If you're interested there's an exercise for beginning to develop this ability in the "Working with" commentary on this card.

At its highest point, the Star marks the massive and irresistible down-rushing of energy which occurs whenever we are able to open ourselves consciously to the powers around us. When we can allow ourselves to become conduits of such energy, we become, albeit unknowingly, lightbearers who flood the world with brightness and colour. In so doing, we become beacons for the good things in life... and they are drawn to us as surely as a moth flies to a flame. Not only do we shower blessings upon ourselves, but we also bring brilliance to others.

Whilst the technique of learning how to do this is demanding, it is worth perfecting the art, considering the amount of miracles we shall make once we have got the hang of it.

Imagine the feeling you might experience if, when you walk into a room, you fill it with the radiance of the light you carry through your life. You will have surely met people who are able, purely by their presence, to introduce such luminosity wherever they go. The ease of spirit and optimism such a presence brings to our world is completely invaluable. Such bright spirits sprinkle all of us with stardust!

THE MOON

Thoth Tarot - The Moon

As you may know, many of the mundane interpretations of this card centre on deceit, illusion, and dishonesty... but the fact that this is what the card reveals is based in the way that people tend to use its inner gnosis, rather than these qualities being inherent to the card itself.

The Moon is about the experience of becoming initiate into the Mysteries – just as Death indicates the act of initiation, the Moon points to the ways in which initiation will change us. Because these changes take place on the inner level of our being, they are hidden from view... secret... private. They are not necessarily obvious to the people around us. Even those closest to us will often miss the subtle shift of mindset that occurs as a person becomes more spiritually aware.

I bet we have all met the sort of person who seems to talk all the time about their apparent spiritual progress...

The fact of the matter is, though, that for the genuine and dedicated seeker, open discussion of their beliefs and discoveries is fairly rare. Students who are moving actively along their life path will not talk indiscriminately about what they are experiencing. They tend to seek out (as thoughtfully as possible) like-minded individuals with whom to share experiences, and they keep a low profile when no such people show themselves.

The study of spiritual matters – whichever your chosen path – is an intensely personal one. Whilst you may find yourself able to compare certain types of milestone notes with others, there will be something completely unique about many of your experiences. It will be shaped by innumerable influences – your initial belief system, your ethical ideals, your own personality, your individual choices. And the further you travel in your explorations the greater will become your sense of 'ownership' of these experiences. In the end they add up to a wealth of hands-on and sometimes hard-won treasure which defines who you are, and where you plan to go next.

This is the effect of initiation, as against the act. It is the ongoing unfurlment of you as a magickal being. Within its confines will grow up your sense of Selfhood, your understanding of where you fit in the world, an honest and realistic assessment both of your strengths and weaknesses. And it's private.

THE SUN

Thoth Tarot - The Sun

Because of the infinitely joyous influence that this card brings in with it, we can allow ourselves to feel warmed by the Universe whenever it appears. Often it's necessary to open ourselves to the power of the great energies which constantly surround us in order to become consciously aware of their effect – but once we have done this, and experienced its value we will find ourselves much more happy to remain 'set to receive' than to shut ourselves down again.

One of the hidden secrets of the Sun card is intimated by its position in the story the Major Arcana tells us about spiritual development (and yes I will write that down one of these days ;-) After the temptation of the Devil, the shock of the Tower, the hope of the Star, the initiation of the Moon, comes the light of the Sun... divine light – the light of revelation, of fresh wisdom, of breakthrough with joy into unknown territory.

Once we commit ourselves to a life of personal spiritual development we will hit these moments over and over again – they are part of peeling the layers of the onion which is life. We call it "the parting of the veils" – that moment when the walls between layers break down, if only momentarily, in order to allow us a brief glimpse of the big picture.

Anybody who has experienced one of these revelationary leaps of perception will never, ever forget it. It will stand as a crucial milestone on their journey toward themselves.

One particularly outstanding revelation I experienced happened when I was running a high fever. I saw two mighty pyramids, one white and slightly translucent, and one black but shiny... they were tumbling in the Void. Slowly, slowly they spun until their bases touched. There was a mighty clang, and suddenly I could see space pouring out of the pinnacles of both of them... stars and planets from the white pyramid and the vast darkness from the black.

I gained a lot of realisations from examining this vision. I understood the necessity for polarity better than I had before; I saw the reflective qualities of creation – you get what you give; the simple truth that so long as light exists, so will darkness... and equally so will some of the more negative things we associate with darkness.

Most versions of the Sun show a mound or hill, with dancing children playing on its flanks. The top of the mound is usually encircled by a fence or wall. As we have seen, the Moon is a card (on the deep level) of initiation into the Mysteries. The Sun's wall depicts the divide which exists between those who take an active role in their own self development, and those who do not. And it also indicates how, with the innocence and trust of children, we can pass safely through the portals into the broader aspects of life's process without fear. Fear belongs below the wall...

I mentioned earlier the idea of drawing on the energies on the Universe – the process is simple: imagine a rainbow hued stream of energy surrounding you, and then take some deep breaths whilst visualising the forces of the Universe flowing into you... the more you practice the better results you will get!! You can do this at any time that you feel stable and comfortable within yourself. Once you become quite experienced you can also try it when you feel quite distressed or turbulent inside – but leave this until you have worked the exercise enough to familiarise yourself with both the action, and its results.

THE AEON

Thoth Tarot - The Aeon

This is a powerful card whose interpretation has expanded quite dramatically over the last century or so. Originally Judgement was said to relate to the life and death cycle, and to the call of awakening that comes for righteous spirits. On a mundane level, it was interpreted as the process of making a judgement, or of applying justice to a given situation.

Whilst these meanings remain, the more spiritual connotations within this card have become increasingly significant. An Aeon is a time frame – a period in which a given ethos emerges, rises and falls. That ethos shapes the society it affects, reaches ascendancy, during which time it permeates all aspects of life, and then it begins to fall away. As it gradually decays, there can often be a period of turbulence and confusion – a time where society appears to begin to break down. There are often increasingly bloody and desperate conflicts during these end times. Dissension is common, and the methods of expressing that dissent will become increasingly cacophonous as the breakdown reaches its height.

But out of this chaos emerges the succeeding Aeon – its ruling credo will be, in some respects, a rebellion against what has gone before, and in others, an affirmation and outgrowth of its predecessor. Gradually a new form of stability develops, bounded by a new set of social rules, beliefs and mores. And thus another Aeon rises out of the ashes like a phoenix. This is the natural pattern of development of spirit. And we poor souls live through it.

The 20th Century, according to many philosophers and spiritual leaders, was the cusp between Aeons. We are now dusting off the ash and attempting to assert that new ethos. No wonder we can sometimes feel a little battered by life. We, in our various ways, are the bricklayers of the new adytum – the first candles lit in an eventual sea of light – the pioneers walking the threshold of the New Age.

It is a bit of a responsibility, is it not? Yet the very fact that we are here proves that we have something worthwhile to contribute. And we have taken the decision to do so – to actively play our part in whatever way we can.

That's the inner revelation of the Aeon!!

THE UNIVERSE

Thoth Tarot - The Universe

As the final Major Arcana card in the Tarot, the Universe opens the door to the minutiae of everyday life and emotion, as detailed in the Minor Arcana. We have passed through each of the archetypes, the high level spiritual development and the ways in which life flows through the Universe, and we have come to the world itself.

The Universe card is like a two-way gate which swings between heaven and earth. It is through this portal we reach out to our gods, however we consider them. And it is also here that we cross the threshold into daily life. Everything splits here from unity into component parts – including ourselves.

In another way, this card can be considered as the natural precursor to the Fool. We have reached a stage of completion when the Universe rules – we have done everything we set out to achieve, and now we need a new direction in which to move forward. How better to achieve this than to take the leap of faith represented by the very first card in the deck?

If we choose this route then we again work our way through the Majors, on a higher arc and with greater understanding. Have you ever had the experience of attempting to read a book which, at the time, goes straight over your head... then at some later point picked the same book up and learned much more than at the first attempt? This happens when we gain insight and experience. Our comprehension is, to a large part, based upon what we already know.

Eventually we are able to lift ourselves far enough away from the mundane to be able to get an overview on our lives. When that happens we will recognise that what seems at first to be a straight journey from birth to death is, in truth, a series of spirals. We pass through similar experiences over and over again, applying the lessons we have learned in between times.

These spirals often go through phases where suddenly a group of apparent tests are placed in our path within a short timeframe – and it is these periods which most acutely contribute to our spiritual growth. They can be times of great pressure and stress... but the more readily we are able to recognise them, the easier it becomes to go for the high ground in order to get the full picture. In so doing, we tend to minimise the trauma of any given group of events, and to apply what we already know to the situation in order to get a desired outcome.

PART II

WANDS

ACE OF WANDS

Thoth Tarot - Ace of Wands

At the deep level of understanding, the suit of Swords represents the formulation of the Will, and the suit of Wands indicates its implementation. It is only by harnessing these two skills that we can direct our lives more consciously, engaging with the energies of the Universe in order to realise our deepest hopes and dreams. A thorough study of the suit of Wands will give us insight about the implementation of Will – an area in which many of us struggle sometimes. I will examine the practicalities involved in future commentaries on these suits... but first we need to get to know them.

The energy behind the Ace of Wands is mighty. On a mundane level we will see it manifest during periods of healing, and times when we create or re-create new lives. It's a fast bubbling energy, bringing an inner sense of exhilaration and excitement - even when we can't work out what we're feeling good about. At times like this, our sense of self will be positive and confident (even if we are usually the most shy person in the town}. The way we will project ourselves will be more outgoing, more interested, more relaxed.

Part of the higher lore connected to the Ace of Wands focuses on developing that sense of buoyancy at will – thereby creating the right environment to paint our lives the colours we choose rather than having to put up with municipal grey. When we set out to focus and direct our Will, we need to have a certain confidence that we will achieve our ends. We need the energy and self-certainty to turn ideas into possibilities – for without this our ideas remain pipedreams, never to be realised, or even truly aspired to.

Aces are all beginnings – the start of a new stream of force. By definition they imply change, different levels of energy and force. Because of this there is a degree of instability – we are changing direction, selecting a new course. At times like this there will always be some doubt, because as we break away from the familiar, and experience the flux of changes, we can feel as though we are standing, stork-fashion, on one leg. One strong gust of wind could send us scuttling back to the 'good old ways'. To have the trust, both in ourselves and in our Gods, to simply allow the force to flow, can be one of the hardest things under the Sun. Yet it is a fact that, in order to truly direct our lives, we first have to surrender the stranglehold of control.

And having mentioned the Sun up there, it's important to point out that the Ace of Wands and the Sun Major are almost inseparable. The Sun indicates the high level of harmony that can be achieved by harmonising with life's forces... the Ace indicates the way that force filters down into daily life.

The first step along the path to achieving direction of your Will comes here, with this Ace. You need to become familiar with feeling buoyant – with believing in yourself and your abilities. Self-esteem and self-confidence are hard-won qualities, and can be damaged by life's bumps and bangs. They are also often misconstrued by others who feel themselves lacking.

A truly confident person will tell you that they do not live life doubt-free and in utter certainty. They have their worries and concerns as much as anybody. What they also have is the belief that, given that they listen to their deepest feelings, observe their under-lying worries, take account of any thorny issues that present them-selves – that given all this, they will make sound decisions, will be respected and liked by those who matter, will achieve their goals and follow their destiny. This wisdom is born of practice, experience and self acceptance. And we can all work to cultivate a healthy sense of it on a minute by minute basis.

First and foremost, the next time you feel joyous, buoyed up, more confident than usual, make time to sit and examine the feeling. Notice how it changes even the very fundamental things like the way you hold your body. Really think about how you feel, how you think, what you do. And try to fix those feelings firmly in your memory so that you can return to them in future days. Practise feeling good about yourself and life. You will have a lot of fun.

TWO OF WANDS

Thoth Tarot - Two of Wands

This card, Lord of Dominion, has a dark side which is not always recognised by readers. At its highest level of interpretation the card indicates achieving a peak of success and achievement – however, as always with Wands, there is a pent-up energy fizzing away in the background which can be dangerous if not contained and directed.

The card indicates the responsibility with which we must approach our everyday thoughts and actions – it is a challenge to us to recognise that every thought we have creates something – and whether we like that something or not, we must surely 'own' it.

The best way I can describe the energy behind this card is to invite you to strike a match. When you first take the match from the box, it is an inert piece of wood with a coating on one end. Only when you strike the match against the box, do you begin to understand its purpose and function.

The 2 of Wands is equivalent in energy to that moment where the match begins to ignite – it is not yet alight, but it is no longer inert either. It is a little fizzing bundle of combustible material. I am sure we have all experienced that accident where the end of the match flies off, uncontained, and burns a hole in the nearest cushion... this is the 2 of Wands.

It is a high level, exuberant, and somewhat dangerous energy, which needs to be harnessed and handled carefully until such time as it has achieved its given purpose. Then it needs to be extinguished safely before it sets fire to something precious.

In a way you might be able to see that there is an almost explosive quality to this card. We have the immense power of the Ace flowing into the narrow channel which is intended to contain and direct the 2. This power is our own Will. If we fail to contain the power within us we shall emerge with metaphorical slightly scorched cushions – and this could be rather more serious than the effects of the match-head on the sofa.

Only by learning to channel our Will in this fashion will we be able to achieve the highest point of the Lord of Dominion's realm – that of ruler of our own destiny.

THREE OF WANDS

Thoth Tarot - Three of Wands

This card's original name was "Lord of Established Strength", and it was often (and still is) interpreted to indicate that an individual has reached a particular position of material stability and wealth through honest effort.

Then Crowley renamed it, when designing the Thoth deck. He called the card Lord of Virtue. And then the confusion started. This is because often we tend to regard virtue as a little old- fashioned and perhaps even limiting. Yet in order for a thing to have virtue it must, of necessity, also have inherent strength.

We all have vast reserves of inherent strength within us. Every one of us will have surprised ourselves by our ability to deal with stress and trauma at some point. But often we only touch our well-springs of strength in difficult times. We can lose sight of the fact that when sufficiently motivated we can get through pretty much anything at all.

Forgetting our own inner godhood can cost us very dear. Failing to remain aware of this mighty part of ourselves means that we lose the ability to work miracles. It is far more beneficial for us and every-body else if we maintain a strong and respectful contact with that part of ourselves which knows how to fly.

If you are reading this and thinking "I don't think I've got one of those" let me tell you, quite categorically, that you are wrong. The way to prove this to yourself is this – search your memory for a time when you surprised yourself completely by responding almost without thought, in a bad situation: when each action flowed smoothly to the next, where you had no time for fear or what-ifs.

Now concentrate on what you can remember of what you did and how you felt. Do not concentrate on the bit where you come back to yourself, having narrowly averted what could have been a disaster... and remember the surprise. Concentrate on the act itself. See how you acted from what we often call pure instinct... that's not pure instinct... that's the highest level of you. It is the part which is supremely confident at all times, who has a balanced and divine view of self, who KNOWS how to handle a situation. That is your godhood. And it's always there.

FOUR OF WANDS

Completion

Thoth Tarot - Four of Wands

There is a strong similarity between this card, and the Major Arcanum Adjustment, or Justice. This comparison comes up most obviously when a person is in a situation where it seems that fair play has gone out of the window, and instead, unjust influence has been brought into play. If you ever get this card coming up when you or your querent is in a nasty situation – perhaps a conflict with another person who has greater power, or a legal wrangle where they have the advantage because of money or specialised knowledge - it is well worth remembering that the 4 of Wands can indicate a satisfactory, though compromised, outcome.

Sometimes we can allow ourselves to be drawn into conflicts which we simply cannot win. And we can tend to become blinkered about what the outcome might mean for us. We believe ourselves to be unfairly treated, and we entrench in the hope that, in the end, justice will prevail. The energy we pour into an unwinnable situation is wasted. If, during periods like that, this 4 turns up, it's worth considering whether you have dug a hole that you might find it difficult to get out of without a very long ladder.

It can be hard to attain objectivity when our emotions are engaged with a given situation. Since we have strong feelings on the topic, we tend to be driven more by those, than by our rationale. But sometimes it pays off to bring to an end an issue which is loaded against us, so that we can direct ourselves more constructively.

There is also a strong similarity between the 4 of Wands and the Universe. The 4 tends to be more gentle in the way that it concludes issues, and more positive in the energy it brings into a situation. This comes, in part, from the fact that this is a pip card (always less powerful in effect than a Major) and also because of the card's link with Chesed, the 4th Sephirah on the Quaballa. One of Chesed's titles is Mercy. Therefore when a given situation is concluded by the 4 of Wands, often we will quickly be able to identify new opportunities and chances coming our way as we bring a given project or situation to a satisfactory conclusion.

In either case, this Wand also brings forward the question of morality again – we must ensure that our actions are rightful and justified. When we are properly aligned with the Will of the Universe we can achieve a great deal of happiness, fulfilment and contentment when this card shows in readings.

FIVE OF WANDS

Thoth Tarot - Five of Wands

Internal conflict is one of the most damning experiences we humans can have. Nobody can beat us in an argument quite as well as we can ourselves – not only do we know our own areas of confusion, weakness and self-doubt, but we read our own logic before it has properly formulated. When we quarrel with ourselves, the outcome is often more easily predicted by past events than by current progress.

This inner discord is one of the deeper revelations of the Lord of Strife. And it is one of the major interferences we encounter when attempting to impress our positive Will upon the Universe. When our inner dialogue is critical and negative, any of our endeavours is going to be proportionately more difficult to execute.

So once again, we must enter the cobwebby corners of our minds and look for things that hinder us. In our previous work with the 5 of Wands, we have attempted to set right the things we were anxious about that troubled us from the past.

We have often discussed the ethical qualities which underpin the suit of Wands. When influenced by this suit, our consciences come under scrutiny. We need to honestly appraise our behaviour, and determine (without judgement) where with hindsight, we may have done better.

It is natural that, as we grow and develop, we will look back on certain events in our lives and disagree with the course of action we selected at the time. This is a perfectly normal result of engaging actively with our own development. To some extent every animal on the face of the planet has this ability as an instinctual component of their make-up. For instance the puppy who puts his paw in the bonfire is liable to decide fairly quickly that this is not the best idea he ever had.

We will all take wrong turnings when we walk this twisting path of ours. Mistakes are an integral part of our learning process. If we don't wander off along a couple of dead end tracks in our journey, we will never know what it is to return to our chosen destiny – and this is one of the mightiest spiritual and emotional experiences we can have. In order to trigger this important event, we must lose our way for a time.

Life unwinds in a series of ascending spirals. We shall meet the same point of the curve again and again – hoping only that we revisit on a higher arc than last time we were here. This means that we will be faced with the same set of events, posing the same kinds of questions. It is easy to interpret seemingly recurrent circumstances as making the same mistake twice. However what is important is the understanding we bring to the repeat performance which tempers our behaviour and alters the situation.

One of the things that can interfere with our process of development is that, from time to time, we will identify periods, actions, behaviours of which we are thoroughly ashamed: times when we feel, in retrospect or at the time, that we let ourselves down. The more we establish a good relationship with our inner spirit, the more easily (unfortunately) are these periods identified. This is because, as we grow, our standards of expected self-conduct become higher and higher. This is a sign of growth, and must not be misinterpreted.

It is important to recognise that the times when you fell to the wayside were as much a part of your journey as the times when you were proud of yourself. Try to practise seeing your mistakes in the light of what you learned from them, rather than punishing yourself. Realise that you are no longer that person. You would face the same decision or choice from a very different standpoint these days... one in which you approve of your own behaviour. You might choose to do the same thing again, with greater insight and self-trust. Or you might choose an entirely different course of action. Either way, hopefully you would be happy with the decision you made. And that is because of how you handled things last time.

SIX OF WANDS

Thoth Tarot - Six of Wands

This is always a welcome card to turn up in a spread. It indicates breakthrough, celebration, and success. However, its title, Lord of Victory, reminds us that no victory is possible without the fight beforehand – and that there will not only be a victor but also a vanquished. It is a strange thing that people often miss the significance of the 'other side' in any battle. For every winner there is a loser.

We tend to place victory in the 'event' category when considering its implication – yet this is probably something of a misunderstanding. To a great extent, victory is the result of a state of mind. If we enter into any conflict believing that we will come off worst, inevitably we will. The application of the human Will is a hard-won skill, but one which, once mastered, serves us well especially in difficult or confrontational situations. If we believe our cause is justified, our standpoint fair, then we are liable to align our Will with our desired end product. When we do this, we stand a very good chance of achieving our ends.

Of course, it is possible to convince ourselves that we are right when we are not – particularly when a situation engages our emotional perspective as well as our reason. We need to be objectively critical of our intentions in this case, to ensure that we apply ourselves only to those things we have a reasonable and rightful expectation of obtaining. The ethical thread which runs through this Suit demands that we do this.

This card brings in a burst of welcome energy when it appears as a Card of the Day, or in a reading. It promises us that, despite current struggles and difficulties, we can succeed so long as we conscientiously dedicate ourselves to our cause. Even when circumstances things appear to deny all resolve, if we are sufficiently determined, and as unwavering as we can be, then we shall eventually attain our goals.

Sometimes, when the card comes up, it marks a clear cut contention – a court case, a formal disagreement, an official complaint. In this case it is quite easy to see the 'enemy' so to speak.

But often the 6 of Wands will come up to mark the required state of mind we need in order to be victorious in more amorphous, or diffuse situations. It could come up to show that we need real dedication to achieve our goal of, say, buying a home, or paying off debt. It could indicate the long term effort we must invest in order to get a given qualification, or the sheer nose-to-the-grindstone endeavour it takes to complete a demanding project.

SEVEN OF WANDS

Thoth Tarot - Seven of Wands

Have you ever considered what kind of courage and commitment it must take to be so dedicated to a cause or belief that you are willing to give up anything in order to support it – even your life?

We tend to think that it takes a special sort of person to exhibit this kind of valour. We regard it as beyond the reach of 'ordinary' people. Yet this is not true. Valour emerges when we are true to ourselves. When we go to the aid of others less fortunate, when we face opposition of our beliefs with grace, honesty and integrity, when we make decisions which mean we will be hurt for doing what we consider to be the 'right' thing, we are valorous.

Life often puts us in a position where we have to make a choice based on ethical structures and beliefs. It is very easy to take the route of least resistance when somebody acts, for instance, in a racially intolerant fashion, when we abhor such behaviour. But if, in this situation, we speak our truth, even when we believe it will probably make no difference, we are valorous.

One thing that often escapes people's notice when considering concepts like this, is that the truly valiant actions are usually undertaken by people who don't want to have to be brave, but know that they must be. They are faced with a situation which they feel to be wrong, and they are compelled to do something about it. They may feel reluctant or hesitant to take action, they may seriously doubt that their voice will be heard. But they act anyway.

We are all capable of showing valour. We may not necessarily believe that we are, until we find ourselves in a situation that demands we go the extra mile. The 7 of Wands comes up to indicate times in which we find ourselves challenged by life, and needing to be true to ourselves, regardless of the cost.

EIGHT OF WANDS

The Lord of Swiftness is the 'light bulb' card. It marks those moments of intense insight, sudden inspiration and revelation that come every now and again. Seemingly intractable problems suddenly yield solutions – original and surprising by nature, yet often having been there, unnoticed all the time.

When the 8 of Wands has influence it is important to listen to apparently unconnected information, because the Universe will do its best to communicate its intentions by any means it can.

Be alert to coincidence, and to those seemingly unimportant comments which, for no good reason, assume additional importance when you hear them. Open yourself up to the energies in your life and allow them to slot into the other experiences you have.

More than anything else, this card relates to lightning speed of thought, when your mind seems to race ahead of itself and you tend to make bold leaps of understanding. Whilst this is happening, often there is no substantiated logic to the patterns of thought – but this tends to become more obvious after the initial onrush has abated.

This card represents Will unfettered. It gives us the ability to lock into the web of Wyrd, enabling us to access the wisdom of the Universe. We will know things we did not know before, sense things with a more acute level of awareness than normally, and we will be more in touch with our intuition.

Whilst the influence itself is often brief, our experiences when affected by the Lord of Swiftness will often form the foundation of life-changing decisions and choices made in the period that follows. Our spiritual perception will forge forward, opening up new areas of exploration before us. We will find it easier to gain an overview.

The sheer passion which abounds with this card carries us forward in fresh directions, lending us temporary courage to face new challenges. And often, once the wave has broken and withdrawn, we shall find ourselves changed beyond measure.

NINE OF WANDS

Thoth Tarot - Nine of Wands

To some extent it could be said that each of the 9s is about preparatory union. The numerological significance of 3 x 3 indicates a growing spiral of smaller achievements leading to the whole integration of given understanding about a particular topic.

The biggest task associated with the Lord of Strength is that of integrating the inner personality. One of the toughest things about integrating your entire personality centres on your ability to identify, acknowledge and accept those parts of you that you do not like very much.

Perhaps our biggest problem when it comes to handling this process is the accepting part. We like to think of ourselves as pretty perfect beings, really. Even the sort of person who deliberately puts themselves down is generally running a personal agenda behind that act that suggests that if they say something nasty about themselves, others will correct them, and in the process say some very nice things.

But even when strategies like this are employed, in the end, we cannot run away from ourselves. There is a focus of light and truth within each one of us which, if given voice, demands that we become all that we possibly can. This part of us plays no hide-and-seek games with personal truth. It sees our entirety, warts, triumphs and all. It has a more realistic view of us than we will achieve until such time as we are willing to open ourselves to it whole-heartedly. When we are willing to stand in light, we are bathed in light. Naturally, light casts a shadow... but that shadow is an integral part of self.

It exists as a 'flight-plan' which allows us to map out the next stage of our journey – eliminating those aspects of Self which appear to serve no further purpose. This business of things no longer serving us well is one that often causes people problems in their self-development.

When we pass through difficult stages in life, we tend to develop strategies and beliefs that protect us and keep us safe as we move through particularly difficult periods. However, if we are honest, we can be very reluctant to drop those strategies when we move beyond the situation in question. There is a great deal of difference between learning from past experiences, and continuing to live within them even though they no longer exist.

When you undergo major life changes – whether these are expressed into life, or felt within your own Self - it is important to spend time clearing away out-dated strategies. A behaviour which is entirely justified and appropriate in one setting could be wholly damaging and destructive in another.

One of the most common areas we seem to make this mistake in is that of love, and its sometimes concomitant pain. When moving through a relationship which disappoints us, fails to live up to our hopes and expectations, hurts us and leads us to feel inadequate, we often find it necessary to withdraw. We concentrate primarily on our own thoughts, needs, considerations and feelings. In the situation, this is entirely necessary. We need to refocus, to see what we will be happy with, and what we will not.

Hopefully, as a result of developing this attitude we find our way into happier, more secure times. We feel that we have kept ourselves safe, whilst determining what our next course of action shall be. But how many of us, having emerged from the dank tunnel of misery, consider whether those same defensive reactions remain, waiting to be triggered? Too few, I suspect.

If we move into another relationship with a set of spikes worthy of an obstacle course designer fencing our most vulnerable emotions, we will be difficult to draw close to. We might be interpreted as cold or calculating by partners who enter willing into the mutual exploration that is attraction.

It is as well that we honestly update our responses in accordance with our experiences – integration comes easier to those of us who are relatively happy with ourselves, than to those of us that experience unresolved disquiet.

TEN OF WANDS

Thoth Tarot - Ten of Wands

The Lord of Oppression usually brings frustration and a sense of ineffectuality when it appears. Often we will find ourselves in a situation which seems to have no satisfactory resolution, or wanting something that it seems we cannot get no matter how hard we try.

Whilst often the answer to this kind of frustration is to simply wait until the time is right, there is a slightly more hidden aspect to the card. This comes about because of the thread of morality that runs through the entire suit of Wands. If we remember, for a moment, that Wands are the suit of Will, the reason that our morality is also stressed when these cards come up will become apparent.

The operation of Will without ethics brings about some of the most evil acts of our race. Even misplaced ethics can cause a great deal of grief and unhappiness – look at the effects of prejudice for example. When a person is prejudiced, they probably will have a set of ethics (however clearly thought out) functioning. Prejudice is not blind. An individual holding prejudice in their hearts about something or somebody will have considered the reason they feel that way – they will have pre-judged the matter in question.

Consider, for a moment, a person with great strength of Will, and absolutely no concern for the consequences of the operation of that Will, save in as much as it will affect them personally. We are looking at a monster in human guise aren't we? So... the secret behind the appearance of the 10 of Wands is this – when you have aligned yourself sufficiently to a given objective, when you have focussed your Will and let it go, and when you still - after patiently waiting and working for your desire – do not see any progress, it's time to consider whether your wish was the right one.

Sometimes the Universe quite simply refuses to give us what we want. It will act to turn back your stream of desire, or disconnect it from the whole. This might be because your desire is going to harm you, because you are choosing the wrong path, or you have Willed something that contravenes your ethical standpoint.

If you find yourself in the frustrating position of having worked REALLY hard for something, and still it hasn't manifested, you need to consider the questions above. Objectively examine whether your intentions were pure, or whether they were coloured by some taint in your thinking. If you're satisfied about your own input, then consider whether there are ways in which what you Willed could harm you. And once you have done these two things and you are contented with the answers you got – then think about the third option – you are, possibly, going in the wrong direction, and the Universe is trying to nudge you back onto your path. There is absolutely no point in resisting this force – it will lead you to a Tower moment if you argue. Best, in this case, you surrender and leave yourself open so that the Universe can give you some useful pointers.

PRINCESS OF WANDS

Thoth Tarot - Princess of Wands

There is a state of mind known in Buddhist and Hindu circles as samadhi. This is a meditative condition which is thought to precede the process of ecstatic union with Godhead (or whatever else you want to call it). The Princess of Wands has strong correspondence with this state – however this is not what we are going to examine today (we'll get to this when I am feeling REALLY erudite).

Instead, we are going to examine one of the things which is regarded as an essential preparation for attempting to enter into samadhi. Very often in our examination of the cards we run into something which can be best described as the Law of Opposites. It is an area which can cause a great deal of difficulty and distress for an ordinary human being, and even more confusion for the spiritual seeker. In some respects, the opposite nature of life seems completely logical, yet its practical workings can perplex us no end.

How, for instance, can you achieve a state of harmony when the world appears to function as a set of contradictions – many of which argue furiously with their neighbours? How do you reconcile the apparent inconsistencies of life and emerge with some kind of coherent overview?

In fact, this area is nowhere near as difficult to interpret as it sometimes appears. The Law of Opposites establishes a given tension in life – a dynamic stressor which allows for forward movement and progress. But we cannot properly understand this stressor if we are unwilling to truly consider and accept the consequences of its function.

We are able to accept certain, obvious indications of the Law of Opposition in action. For instance, we accept that night follows days in a repetitive cycle. We adjust our behaviour, our life patterns, in accordance with the level of natural light we experience. But even here we do our best to cheat nature – we make false light to illuminate the darkness, so that our activities are less curtailed than they would have been when the only light to which we had access was the night sky itself. So even this is a grudging acceptance of the Law.

We accept that Winter is the opposite of Summer. Then once again, we attempt to force Nature to follow our desires, by inventing heating, houses, winter wardrobes, thermal underwear. Even with the most powerful of natural cycles we have only limited acceptance that our lives are governed by certain absolutes.

It is this limited acceptance, and the subsequent value judgement that grows from it, that causes most of our problems when we attempt to understand the principle of opposing forces in our Universe. We lose the ability to simply accept. There is not a single naturally occurring phenomenon on our planet that we have not attempted to improve upon – sometimes with dire consequences.

One of the integral processes in preparing for the state of samadhi is to learn how to identify, name and reconcile opposing stresses within the being. These are not only considered on the spiritual levels – they filter right the way through the being taking into account the emotions, thoughts, beliefs, attitudes and physical actions and mannerisms that define (for instance) you as a unique individual.

You can begin this process in one way which will subsequently prove very helpful. This is an exercise that, if followed through on a regular basis, will pull into sharp focus the contradictions that exist within yourself. In the course of one day, you probably find yourself often thinking or saying a thing, and then almost instantly following up with a thought that begins: yes, but...

As much as you can, write down every instance you note of self-contradiction. Don't judge either aspect. Simply start keeping a record. Those inner arguments form the basis of your personal stressors. The more you know about them, the easier they become to either reconcile, or reformulate.

PRINCE OF WANDS

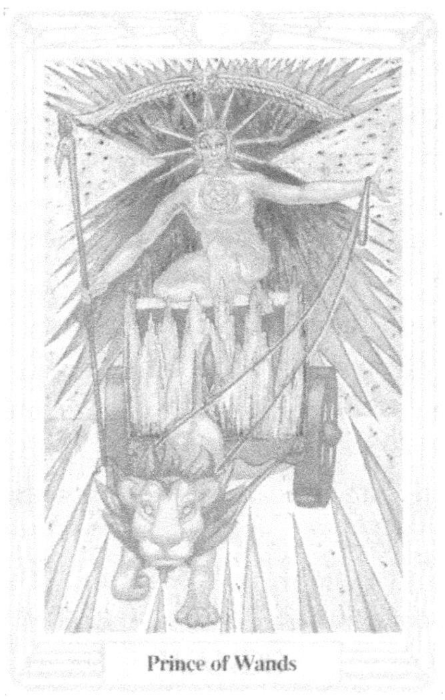

Thoth Tarot - Prince of Wands

I have touched upon the morality which runs through the suit of Wands often before – this suit helps us to develop a strong ethical code and a firm sense of what is 'rightful' in terms of our human endeavour. In a world as tempting as ours, we need a clear understanding of what we see to be a good set of principles to live by.

The Prince of Wands is regarded as the guardian of our ethical history. If you accept the principle of reincarnation, then you may have examined the concept of Karma at some point. I have always regarded Karma as the record of our own behaviour toward ourselves, others and godhead, however we see that.

Sometimes people present the process of Karma as a very cut-and-dried tit-for-tat procedure – x does something nasty to y, and then in the next life y comes along and does the same thing to x. I do not agree with that kind of simplistic view of Karma. To me, this force is as much a tool we are afforded in our journey through life, as are our books.

However, I digress. (Who me? Never!)

In our struggles to reach for the perfection within, we learn and develop in accordance with our experiences. The more open we become to the natural forces of the Universe, the more we see ourselves change and grow. We probably also release more of our own innate power.

Therefore the requirement for a strong ethical code becomes progressively more important. Since we are liable to be in fortunate positions – possibly with a lot of power and responsibility – we need a highly developed sense of how we wish to conduct ourselves. This needs to be examined and updated often. And we need to be entirely honest with ourselves.

Whether you agree that we live progressive lives, or whether you think that this opportunity comes only once, you will learn a great deal from examining your ethical history. Look back over your life and pick out an event which occurred that you now know you would not allow to occur again. There is a good chance that looking back will make you wince – but beyond the wincing is some extremely valuable information to be had about yourself.

Consider why you would not act the way you did back then. Chart the changes that have happened to you, which have acted to shift your point of view. You will find a thread which records the growth that you have made. And once you can see that, perhaps you can also accept why you acted as you did then... and if necessary forgive yourself.

QUEEN OF WANDS

Thoth Tarot - Queen of Wands

Because of their connection with the element of Fire, Wands contain a vast resource of passion. The Queen of Wands can be interpreted as the Mother of this enormous well of loving energy. Her influence is that of well-channelled force, directed at growth both in herself and in others. She can act as a source of invaluable support and sustenance.

This wellhead of love half-cloaks a very important understanding about the Queen of Wands... rather like the woman who rides the lion in the Lust/Strength card, she is in love with life. She enjoys all of her experiences, and wrings from them the positive, the happy, the meaningful with a determination which can be completely breath-taking. She is an incurable optimist with a bright slant on life however it treats her.

Have you ever noticed that people who live their lives in love with the experience seem to receive more in the way of enjoyable surprises, lucky breaks and general good fortune, than those who live with their eyes focussed firmly on the floor? I think this is because life loves a lover... and a lover of life is probably more welcome than any other.

It can sometimes be very difficult to love life, can't it? When we're feeling embattled, fragmented or hurt it can be hard to remind ourselves that life is a miracle. Despite the fact that these are entirely natural responses, they do not really do us too much good. Our negativity tends to follow us around like a dark cloud, attracting the darkness of others to us as surely as moths fly to a flame.

It can be very hard to re-orient our attitudes when we are feeling unhappy or downhearted. It can be onerous to look for the happy spots in a quagmire of depression. Yet in the end product it is precisely that type of determination that will drag us through the nasty times, and lead us back out into the sunshine...

It is worth bearing in mind that the Queen of Wands can make this task much easier. Meditation on the card during hard times, or even simply fixing the card on a wall somewhere that you will see it often, will help you to feel that you are not alone in your struggles.

KNIGHT OF WANDS

Thoth Tarot - Knight of Wands

Have you ever wondered how it is that you can pour your Will out into the Universe and have your desires manifest – often in ways you had not quite envisaged? Any person who is attempting to take control of their own destiny will, eventually, experience the peculiarly synchronistic effect that life can have sometimes. And any experienced practitioner of magickal working will probably have a wealth of anecdotes to share – many amusing, and some, warnings from the wise.

The fact of the matter is that, in the manifestation of Will, we must determine that there is no such thing as coincidence – there is only synchronicity – the coming together of certain apparently unconnected events which, in their entirety, work toward your desired intent.

When we throw directed (or indeed, undirected) thoughts into the Universe they seek out that which is similar to them. You could, if you chose, visualise this as a web or network of tiny streams of energy, each of which has a focussed purpose. This web is infinitely complex and inter-related, with many crossing points, where different types of energy connect. Your wishes look for the relevant strands and attach themselves to them... and then they need to find other threads which can create your new reality for you. Eventually... with all the relevant strands plaited into a chain of Will, your request comes flowing back to you and begins to manifest... often in a stream of, on the surface, random events.

There are many names for this web, or energy flow. The one I tend to use most often originates from the Anglo Saxon language... Wyrd. This is the root word that gave birth to our common usage weird. It is pronounced somewhere between word and weird... if you can imagine that.

My understanding of this complex network of energy is that when I throw my Will into the Universe, it touches upon many strands of the web of Wyrd, carrying my desires to the Higher Powers – who then decide if I know what's good for me. Some people don't ascribe to a Higher Deity of any sort, yet they still use the web to create what they want. It does not seem to matter what you actually believe in – the process still works.

But it can create some interesting twists and turns along the journey. That is why the question of intent is so crucially important when you begin. We need to be quite sure we have considered all the implications of the manifestation of our desire before we let rip – otherwise, we'll end up with a collection of anecdotes as well.

What does all this have to do with the Knight of Wands? One of his hidden titles is that of Master of the Web of Wyrd. When he is influencing your life, look carefully for two things – synchronous events which appear to nudge you in the right direction, and indications that you are moving closer to your current goal. These may well come in the form of 'life talking to you'. A stranger will make a comment which seems, for no apparent reason, to carry enormous import from your perspective. A billboard will carry a significant advert. The music you hear, the programmes you watch, the things people say will somehow serve to instruct you, or to clear your path. Odd random coincidences will occur which point you in the right general direction.

When these things happen and you have no specific intent in mind, they might be the whisper of your intuition, guiding you or informing you. Listen well when this Knight is abroad... he allows life to talk back to you.

PART III

CUPS

ACE OF CUPS

Thoth Tarot - Ace of Cups

One of the deeper aspects of the Ace of Cups covers the whole area of intuition – its development, its interpretation, and the uses to which we put it. Some people have very sharply honed intuition upon which they have come to rely extensively. But for others it tends to be a hard won skill.

There are many different ways in which you can increase your intuitive levels. One surprisingly useful process is to take a little quiet time early in the morning before your day really gets started, and ask yourself "What does my intuition tell me about today?" Note anything that pops into your head, and then just carry on as normal. You may well get confirmation of one of those fleeting thoughts as the day moves on.

There's a fine line between identifying intuitive input, and imagining what will happen. Intuition tends to be very random, and often unexpected. Imagining generally follows a reasonably logical train of thought. So put greater attention on the off-the-wall thought than on a chain of interlinked ideas. Do not forget, though, that the chain reaction can be caused by intuition in the first place. As always, keep notes. You need to keep a record of your thoughts here in order to check your reliability especially in the early stages of learning how to listen to your "still inner voice".

Why is intuition so important when reading Tarot? Because it helps you to select, from the vast array of interpretational possibilities, the correct understanding of a given combination of cards. Many people, when first beginning to read the Tarot, can feel intimidated when they consider the job of attempting to commit to memory the meanings of all 78 cards, not to mention learning how each affects another when it appears in a spread.

Whilst a certain amount of sheer hard work is necessary in the early stages, once a person has got to grips with the general meaning of each card, having well- developed intuition will assist enormously as the reader progresses. So it is as well to work on listening to the 'still inner voice' as often and as thoughtfully as you can to encourage it to speak up more often.

TWO OF CUPS

Thoth Tarot - Two of Cups

Not surprisingly, this card, the Lord of Love, deals with that mighty human emotion – we crave it, fear it, yearn for it, despise it, pine for it, loathe it... as yet, we have not found another topic to immerse ourselves in as totally as we can immerse ourselves in the topic of love.

Our lives often circle around the giving and receiving of love, the understanding of love, the expression of love in an endless dance which is both immensely fulfilling and indescribably painful. If we were to spend a single day writing down each and every thought we had, whether directly or indirectly connected with love, we should not find time to do anything else. Try it if you do not believe me – and do not forget to note the brief smile at the lovers on the corner, the sense of loneliness when a particular song plays, the passing contemplation of sex with a lover. You will not keep up with your own mind.

The 2 of Cups relates specifically to intimate love – the kind we reserve for partners. In truth this is probably the type of love that causes us the most heartache – but it can also bring us true realisation of self, an explicit understanding of who we are at the deepest reaches of our being.

Whilst the love we feel for friends and family is abiding, and hopefully, nourishing, it is a less turbulent thing (by and large) than intimate love. I think this is because, in intimate love, we surrender a very vulnerable and fragile part of ourselves to our partners. Whilst we express this part of ourselves primarily in making love, this delicate underbelly is far more extensive than this.

Our belief systems tell us that, when we are in love, we shall be able to share our deepest and most well-defended secrets with our partner, our confidante. We want them to do the same. Yet it is this exact belief which can cause a great deal of grief and pain. Two individual human beings cannot, and should not, merge into one.

Our relationships are strong and enduring as much for the differences they celebrate between the two people, as they are for the similarities. Can you imagine how swiftly you would become bored with a partner who always agreed with you, never had a differing point of view to you, never brought new ideas and experiences to the relationship? If you consider carefully what it is that first attracts you to a potential mate you will find that the magnetism between you rests on a complex and infinitely varied bunch of opposites and likenesses.

So, what of our urge to enter into total union with another? I have touched on this with the two earlier commentaries about the Lord of Love. The one being on the face of this planet that you can healthily enter into absolute union with is yourself. To merge the active conscious with the dreams of the sub-conscious, the input of the psyche, the open glow of spirit is to enter into and reside within your own soul. There are depths to you which you have never explored. Get to know yourself as a new friend... respect your knowledge, appreciate your skills, observe your flaws... just as you would another person. I guarantee you that if you give yourself this freedom, you will discover parts of yourself you never knew existed – and it is this for which you truly yearn.

THREE OF CUPS

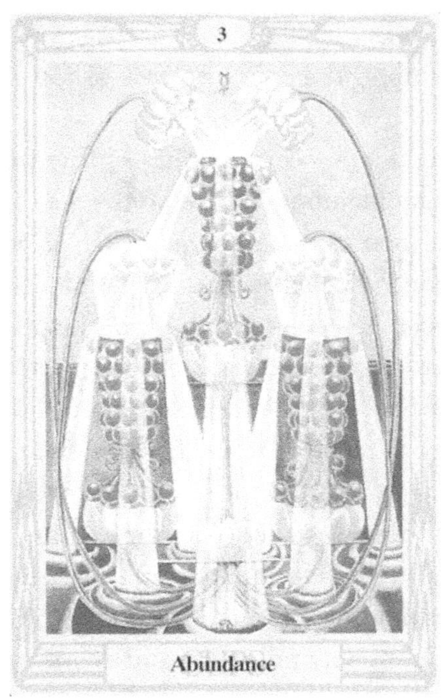

Thoth Tarot - Three of Cups

When working on the commentary for the Lord of Abundance in the Working With series I suggested a brief breathing exercise which was intended to help you to establish a clear link with the generous energies of the Universe. This is because this card encapsulates the river of eternal and infinite power which consistently flows through our lives, into which we can tap at any time we choose.

This is an amazingly joyous, warm card, filled up with buoyant celebration and exhilaration. On many versions of the card, the illustration depicts three female figures dancing together. And herein we discover one of the underlying mysteries of the cards numbered 3 in the Minor Arcana.

Each of these cards – Sorrow, Virtue, Works and Abundance – represents a concept called the Triple Goddess. It is amazing how often this concept occurs throughout many differing belief systems in the world. One of the most familiar interpretations may be that of Virgin, Mother, Crone which crops up in pagan belief systems. This one is dependent upon the aging process of a woman through the stages of her life.

In others systems, you see the group of three women indicating the same series of momentous changes in the life of any woman – her time as a maiden, then as a mother, and then as an older and more experienced woman, reflected again and again.

There is a special power and strength in the principle of womanhood that is often overlooked, and even denigrated. The roles of nurturer, gatherer, creatrix and watcher over the dying and dead have, in mythology, been given to the female of the species from time immemorial. In some ways, these roles have been misdirected, and pulled out of alignment by society over thousands of years... however this does not undermine their function and relevance – it only undermines our understanding of them as archetypes which define a certain amount of our own underlying and divine nature.

Goddesses are, by no means, weak. Contemplate the awesome power of Sekhmet, Lioness deity of the Egyptians. The myths surrounding her are full of mystique, power and indisputable strength. In many ways, she can be described as a destructive force, but she is also fierce guardian of 'rightful truth'.

Women, like the goddesses they reflect into everyday life, are creatures of great and enduring strength. When set in their appropriate position against the backdrop of life, they fulfil a role every bit as important and essential as their male counterparts.

I have never ascribed to the viewpoint that human beings, regardless of their gender, are the same. I think in our unaltered state, without the fashionable constraints of current society, there are innumerable differences between the male of the species, and the female. And the differences complement each other. The concept of the battle of the sexes is a manmade (or possibly woman-made) construct which does nothing to further our appreciation of the might and grace of our race. Rather it detracts from a balance which should be symbiotic, not contentious.

The Lord of Abundance refers primarily to the female flow of energy into the world. There are Wand cards (specifically the 2) which refer more to the male flow of energy into the world.

FOUR OF CUPS

Thoth Tarot - Four of Cups

The principle of pleasure is a complex one at the best of times, and is further mystified by our complex societal attitudes toward it. With the introduction of the pleasure/pain concept, our understanding of pleasure has become ever more shrouded in half-truths.

The Lord of Pleasure addresses this complicated mix of feelings, and attempts to make plain that which has disappeared under a heap of misconceptions. Anyone would think that the very idea of pleasure was, by definition, something purely attributed to sexual gratification these days – the word itself has become synonymous with sexual acts, if you are to believe my inbox.

Yet pleasure stems from the root "to please". That which pleases you brings you pleasure. When we approach the idea behind this card from this perspective the concept becomes a lot clearer. Anything that pleases you is pleasurable. And feeling pleasured is pleasant – sure this can apply to sex, but it can apply to a very broad range of experiences.

When I discussed this card at the Working With level I was talking about how we have a peculiar habit of not valuing the love of those we see as unattractive as highly as the love we experience from those who are attractive to us. This has arisen, in part, I suspect, from the sexualisation of love as an emotion.

We must strive toward purity of interpretation when considering our feelings of pleasure, deliberately separating it from society's somewhat twisted understanding. That way we engage more deeply with pleasure when we experience it, and in so doing we feed our souls with an openness of spirit that might otherwise be obscured from view.

FIVE OF CUPS

Thoth Tarot - Five of Cups

One of the most important skills we need to develop in life is the ability to own our pain. Sometimes we go to extreme lengths to attempt to avoid accepting disappointment and loss – and the very avoidance procedures we employ can often cause even more difficulties in their own right.

Denial can rob us of the ability to draw upon our inner resources in order to convert pain into useful lessons. It can stop us from developing a well-rounded view of our own coping procedures, and as a result, of having any faith in our strength and resilience. It can lead us to feel helpless and victimised. We surrender a vast amount of personal power when we get into this cycle.

Reality, whilst sometimes painful, can also be joyous, affirmative and supportive. To face what actually exists in our lives gives us the opportunity to address what needs our attention, rather than wasting our time phantom-fighting in the fear zone.

Many of us will have experienced, at one time or another, the massive leaps of spiritual understanding that can occur as we pass through periods of intense pain. Not only do we learn more of the unseen in life during these times, but we also gain a clearer view of ourselves and how we live our lives. Great revelations about the human spirit can emerge during the darkest and most damning of our experiences. But they will only happen if we are willing to feel our emotions without judgement or distortion.

Pain is an inherent part of human life. It does not have to be more fearsome, more disabling, more threatening than any other emotion we shall experience. We might not like it very much – but then we don't much like having teeth pulled until afterward when the discomfort has disappeared.

Oddly enough we tend to respond to emotional pain in a completely different fashion than we respond to physical pain. For instance, how long would you walk around on a broken leg before taking yourself off to the hospital? And once you have had your leg reset, how often would you poke it about and hammer on the splint just to see if you could hurt it some more? If we treated our heart's pain more like a broken leg which can be tended, and will heal, rather than the most terrifying monster we can ever face, perhaps we would take some of the sting out of cards like the 5 of Cups.

SIX OF CUPS

Thoth Tarot - Six of Cups

Surrendering to pleasure, and truly engaging with it, is an art that needs to be practised by most people these days. Yet when we are able to really connect with those things that pleasure us, we are more alive and excited than ever. This card is the exact opposite of the one which precedes it – the Lord of Disappointment – and yet the lesson does not change. When we talked about that card we were examining owning our own pain in order to learn from it – the Lord of Pleasure is about owning our own sensual nature for exactly the same reason.

How often do you give yourself the time to pause and really fill up your eyes with beauty, and allow your heart to brim with appreciation? How often in the course of one day do you simply stop and enjoy the sensation of being alive? If you are like most people, your answer to those two questions will be "Not as often as perhaps I could".

The human being is blessed with an infinitely complex sensate system. We each have a vast resource of ways in which we can engage with our surroundings. We are capable of discerning the most subtle shifts and changes in our environment. Yet rarely do we give ourselves the time to examine these. Rather we tend to take each of our senses for granted.

Try this exercise now, to remind yourself of the sheer volume of information being fed to you by your senses each day... pause and really look at what your eyes are showing you. As you examine what is probably a familiar environment, notice the wide variety of tones and colours you can see. Look at the shapes and patterns around you. Revel in your ability to discern different objects.

Then try the same thing with your ears... listen carefully to what you can hear. Listen to all the noises you usually filter out. Then repeat again with your nose... what can you smell? Touch the different things around you and think carefully about the information your fingertips feed into your brain.

You are something of a walking miracle aren't you?

SEVEN OF CUPS

Thoth Tarot - Seven of Cups

The Lord of Debauch always carries warnings about getting carried away on a physical and sexual level, when he appears in a reading. We find ourselves unable to make solid choices under his influence – wavering and vacillating till we make ourselves dizzy. This confusion and indecision comes primarily from the fact that this card is water-based, elementally, whilst 7s (Quabbalistically) correspond with the Sephirah of Netzach, which elementally speaking is earth-based. Water and earth are passive elements, driven by emotion and deep-rooted passion – but the lack of active elements means that, at times, we can find ourselves flapping about like beached seagulls.

It is rare, these days, that we give any great thought to the way in which lasting intimate relationships develop. This is a shame, and is reflected in the number of agonisingly painful breakdowns that occur in this area of life. Before we began to see sex and love as inter-changeable, the growth of relationships was viewed quite differently.

It was accepted and understood that from the moment two people met each other, that each had the potential to glamour the other. Glamours fall into the realm of the 7 of Cups, so it's as well that we examine them carefully.

So... what exactly is a glamour? In the occult sense it is a bewitch-ment, or enchantment. Some people have naturally high levels of ability to glamour, whilst others learn to do this – often as a by-product of developing confidence and Will. Unfortunately, glamour also tends to be well-developed in highly manipulative people who will use their charms in order to achieve their own ends regardless of the consequence for others.

We have all been glamoured at some point in our lives – beguiled by beauty, enthralled by a person's words, mesmerised by a given atti-tude. It happens a lot at the beginning of a relationship – we fall under the spell of a person only recently met, and find all our emotions tied up in thoughts of them. Our thoughts are focussed on the one topic, and our ability to concentrate on other things flies out of the window.

People often make the mistake of imagining that this captivation is something far more than it usually turns out to be. Once the infatuation begins to wear off, we need something much deeper and more enduring to happily share our lives in contentment and fulfilment with a partner. This is where love comes onto the scene.

I have never believed in love at first sight. When somebody tells me that this happened to them, I quietly wonder whether what they actually mean is that they were in lust at first sight, and from that passion grew the sturdy, ineffably strong power of real love. This is the kind of love that makes you want to grow old with somebody, gathering around you a wealth of change, growth and experience which creates a shared history, and a whole heathland of common ground.

EIGHT OF CUPS

Indolence

Thoth Tarot - Eight of Cups

When I was discussing this card in the Working With section, I touched on a particular matter to which most of us pay scant attention – energy leakage. In our busy lives, this is an ongoing problem, and one which we tend to put to one side as unimportant. That, however, is a serious mistake. Any uninvited drain on our energy is an invasion of our personal space, and is disrespectful.

The trouble is that most people who are prone to feeding on the energies of others are not consciously aware of their actions. They are, nonetheless, acting in a vampiric fashion. This is a learned behaviour which, whilst inherent to the nature of humanity to some extent, can be exaggerated until the recipient becomes a danger to those people around them.

How shall we deal with this? First and foremost, we need to recognise that energy drainers are not extraordinary, nor that they necessarily have any intent to harm. Often, these are needy, dependent people who are vulnerable and in need of support. We have all been there at some time or another in our lives. And the fact of the matter is that our race, in its purest form, may be conceived as part of one organism – the Life Wave. Exchanges of energy are a perfectly natural part of our interaction.

The problem arises when a person fails to recognise that they can generate personal energy, thereby contributing to the Life Wave, rather than consistently acting as a drain upon its resources. There are many reasons that an individual will develop this belief system – usually it results from some kind of disempowerment. This often happens in early life, and will be accompanied by feelings of inadequacy, insecurity and lack of confidence.

People who drain can be perfectly nice people – even painfully nice – the sort that provoke intense guilt if we have to refuse a request. But these people are no less dangerous than the bully type who snatches energy whether or not you agree to it.

Of course right at the top of the pyramid, there are those people who deliberately extract energy. These people are calculating, often psychotic to some extent, and usually very clever in the methods they use.

We have every right to protect ourselves against all of these people. One method is to use the Aura Exercise so often it becomes second nature to you. So long as a tiny part of your consciousness is trained to consistently monitor your aura, and what is impacting upon it, you will become alert to an energy drain as soon as it happens. You will then be able to take corrective action. By strengthening the outer edge of your aura and turning it electric blue, you will be able to repel boarders far more effectively than you might at first imagine.

Once you get the hang of caring for your aura, you will have the additional benefit of finding it much easier to deliberately reach out to establish a connection with those you care for, watch over, and wish to assist in some way. The technique will also help you to develop protected and effective psychic work.

So... off you go to learn and practise the aura exercise!

NINE OF CUPS

Thoth Tarot - Nine of Cups

The Lord of Happiness has the inner title of the Wish Card. When this card is dominant it indicates a great period where you can impress your Will upon the Universe. Coincidentally one thing I have noticed when I draw this card for the card of the day, it is often during the first few days of a New Moon – which is also a very good time for directed acts of Will.

We wish for things all the time... when we daydream, when we wonder, when we are subject to any sort of external stimulus... but we rarely aim at wishing in a way that is likely to make our dreams come true. There is a process known as creative visualisation which can make our wishing much more effective and beneficial if we employ it.

Mind you, like most skills, it takes a bit of practice to begin with. One method I found very helpful when attempting to develop my visualisation techniques was to a take a common object and examine it, very carefully. Then I would put the object down, and close my eyes. I would try to imagine every single detail of the object – checking against the real thing from time to time. I often surprised myself by discovering this process is not as easy as it sounds.

Try this – take, for example, a ballpoint pen and study it very carefully. Look with detail at the barrel, the design, any writing on it, then try to visualise it in your mind. When you compare your imaginal pen against the real thing, take note of things you forgot, or could not create in your mind's eye. And then try again.

What is the point of this exercise? To help you to strengthen your ability to visualise what you want in your life, in detail. That way, when you wish, you will be able to visualise your wish – or the result of your wish, more clearly, more effectively. Being able to do this means that, when you throw your wish out into the Universe, empowered by your Will and longing, you give the High Powers a clearly defined blueprint of what you actually want to materialise. I could tell you numerous amusing (and not so amusing) tales of what happens when a hazy desire is cast for recreation. It is as well to get your aims properly sorted out in advance.

TEN OF CUPS

Satiety

Thoth Tarot - Ten of Cups

At the heart of this card, Lord of Satiety, is the knowledge that we are exactly where we need to be, in our lives, in our environment, and in our spiritual journey. It is a deeply philosophical and joyous card, indicating a state of equilibrium and balance. When this card rules, we are at peace with ourselves and our world.

It is not often that we manage to achieve a sense of profound spiritual peace and 'rightness' with life. But on those rare moments when we do, we need to deeply savour the sense of spiritual bliss we experience. In this way, we store a memory of harmony which we can use to help us return more easily to the state of mind at will.

When we feel like this, all our senses are heightened and empowered. The things we see, we see in greater detail, and with more affinity than at other times. If we spend time filling our eyes with beauty and stillness we will hear more clearly, especially the still inner voice, so we can strive to learn from it and to internalise the truths it speaks to each of us.

We need to be ready to listen for our intuition too. It will be more active and accurate than it is in everyday life. This is because under the influence of this card, and in this state of mind, our upper chakras are able to open more efficiently and align with the Universe more thoroughly. We will find we feel things more deeply, and we can expect great surges of love and appreciation,

Ask yourself "What it would be like to feel this way all the time?" Fear simply cannot compete with these all encompassing emotions so make sure you get the flavour of that experience too.

Above all, enjoy your own self. Rediscover the beauty within you, the strength and power that is yours by right. In so doing, you will make it easier to carry that insight into everyday life.

PRINCESS OF CUPS

Thoth Tarot - Princess of Cups

I've talked a great deal about the process of manifesting dreams when writing about the Tarot – this is because there is an art to getting what you want out of life without interfering with the rights of others. The Princess of Cups is one of those cards that allow you to hope for the highest possible wishes you hold dear to come true.

She brings beauty and grace into our lives, along with the innocence which allows us to reach for the stars without expecting the Moon to get in our way. In some respects she solidifies that which is as yet fluid and transparent, allowing us to see reality – albeit through rose tinted glasses sometimes. She represents the boundless and fearless energy which comes with feeling love in its unadulterated form.

When we fall in love we can do anything. We are filled with joy and exuberance. We feel beautiful, find laughter in everything, view our lives with a sense of unfettered freedom which enables us to climb every mountain, walk every mile. Life itself shines with glory. And our beloved is the focus of our attention. We glow from within. And life treats us well.

If we were able to live in that state regardless of whether we had a significant other we would gain more from every day than we could possibly imagine. Life loves a lover... and responds to one with great enthusiasm and attention. Good things flow to those who feel good. It is true that like attracts like in this world of ours.

Of course this is all very well, but it doesn't help at all if we happen to be passing through a sad, lonely time. In fact, it can exacerbate the misery we already feel, leading us to believe that we shall never be contented again – if all we feel is sadness, then surely we shall attract more of the same to our lives.

To an extent this is true. But we can struggle, even in the saddest times, to break through and catch a glimpse of sunny days. And every single time we do that we make a promise to ourselves of future ease.

We can find momentary joy even when life seems to be dealing us bitter blows – simply by pausing and finding something – anything - in which to take pleasure. In one respect this is how we finally climb out of a pit of despair, by stringing together moments of beauty.

When we do this consciously we create a new openness into which the force of the Universe can flow – if only for a second.

So whether you are happy, sad or somewhere in-between, make today a day when you pause and seek out beauty, romance, harmony and love. Little by little those moments will join together into a stream of contentment.

PRINCE OF CUPS

Thoth Tarot - Prince of Cups

The Prince of Cups has a lot to teach us about the law of supply and demand, and how this applies to deliberate acts of directed Will. Because all acts of Will are powered by our own desire, it is important that we have a strong wish for something, before we begin to direct our Will toward it. If we would rather like something, we will be far less effective in attempting to bring it into our lives than when we want it wholeheartedly, with all of our being.

Never waste your energy going after something that you mildly desire – unless you are simply practising, of course. Rather, engage your Will in the really important things you want to manifest in your life. Your actions will be empowered by your passion, so be sure you have plenty of it about the thing you work for.

How do you decide whether you REALLY want something? How do you separate your less important dreams from your deepest desires? You listen to yourself. It is a strange thing that people think they know what they want... but they sometimes clutter up their true desires with a lot of jumbled thoughts. For instance, if you desperately need to pay the rent this month, and you dream of being wildly rich, it is the rent you should be directing your acts of Will toward. Aiming to be miraculously wealthy is by no means an impossible aim, but it needs to be thought through carefully. In the meantime, your energy will best serve you by making sure you have a roof over your head next month.

As an aside, if you do want to work toward being wealthy, you need to break the process down into stages – this is one of the mountains we discuss when considering the Prince of Disks. Larger aims need careful strategy.

The Prince of Cups signifies the passion we hold around a given topic or person. He is master of passion and desire, and can teach us a great deal about learning to listen to our own needs, focus on available means of fulfilling them, and channelling our most heartfelt desires in order to get what we want out of life.

Then, of course, we need to examine those desires through the lens of the Prince of Wands in order to assess whether what we want is moral, good for us, and within our ethical code.

From this you will see that, at this level, the Princes are very much action cards. They relate to what we do and why we do it – in contrast to Princesses, which at this level are more like idea cards.

QUEEN OF CUPS

Queen of Cups

Thoth Tarot - Queen of Cups

At an inner level the Queen of Cups indicates the priestess who silently resides within all women. It is sometimes said that this priestess serves Isis – the archetypal Egyptian Goddess who was mother, wife, enchantress, sorceress and mage.

This is an ethereal part of our existence – the place in which we can reside between the worlds, taking the unseen to be as real and tangible as the material world. It is the place into which we move during deep meditation, during inner contemplation, and sometimes during prayer and reverence.

It is an essential, yet largely overlooked, integral part of our female state – the male equivalent is that of priest. Yet when we allow ourselves to access this hidden part of Self some wonderful things occur. We begin to truly identify the unique power of woman – that graceful, enduring strength which flows endlessly when it is unhindered.

The Universe is pure energy. When we learn how to connect to certain strands of that energy and allow it to incorporate us into its endless journey, we are lit with its individual qualities and matchless forces – these become part of our consciousness, part of ourselves. And when that happens we are able to move closer to our spirits, and to live life from a perspective which enables us to sense the broader view – to live from the high ground.

The ability to contact the Queen of Cups within provides us with an opportunity to release the totality of our womanliness, in the deepest sense of the word. We can become living goddesses, blessing our worlds by the very fact of our presence.

KNIGHT OF CUPS

Thoth Tarot - Knight of Cups

You may have heard the quote "Love under Will shall be the whole of the Law". It is a statement that was made by Alistair Crowley (don't run away – he did talk some common sense) which sums up the relationship between (among other things) the emotions and the human Will.

The quote has often been misinterpreted as an excuse for licentiousness... but in this particular respect I think Crowley has been even more misrepresented than usual. What he was actually trying to say is that we can only efficiently operate the Will when the emotions, thoughts and spiritual inclinations are aligned.

The Knight of Cups is Lord of Waves and Water – the element of water not only deals extensively with our feelings, but to a slightly lesser degree, and with Earth, it rules our instinctual drives.

You can learn a great deal about the emotions by studying water. Their surface can be ruffled by your thoughts, as the ocean's surface is whipped by the wind. They flow to fit any shape you choose to pour them into, and fit every single crevice, just as water does when poured into a container. When the emotions cease to flow, they can turn rank and bitter, just as water turns stagnant in the same circumstances. Emotions are mutable, changeable, in some respects formless, as is water.

With love almost universally recognised as one of the 'greater' emotions, Crowley's statement begins to make more sense. When our love of life, our love of self, our love of others is balanced, we are motivated in positively and channelled ways toward our desires.

When our passion is girded by love, it becomes an enormous powerhouse of strength and direction. If we are able to breathe the strength of our passion into the channels through which our love flows, then we provide ourselves with an undeniable flow of energy which, when directed by the Will, brings about our most dearly held wishes. Here we find the activated power of prayer; the mighty cry to the High Powers from the heart, which can work miracles.

PART IV

SWORDS

ACE OF SWORDS

Thoth Tarot - Ace of Swords

You will have already gathered in our ongoing discussions about applying your Will, that for this to work the way you want it to, you will need to get to know and accept yourself very well.

It's a strange-but-true fact that many people know their partners, friends and family better than they consciously know themselves. We take ourselves for granted, and do not invest the same level of time and effort getting to know what we really think and feel about certain issues. In fact, we can even go into denial about some topics rather than face up to their effect upon us.

Yet, in order to properly apply the directed Will, we must know ourselves better than any other person in the Universe. If we do not acquaint ourselves thoroughly with our inner life, we stand a fair chance of having our work backfire on us – or go horribly wrong.

So the inner wisdom of the Ace of Swords is to know ourselves. If we use the cutting edge of the sword to clean up the clouds that over-familiarity inevitably creates, we stand a chance of seeing ourselves as we truly are.

I think one of the reasons that people avoid getting to know themselves is because they are not sure they are going to like what they find when they do. It is astonishing how many people can give a long list of weaknesses and faults, and usually a considerably shorter list of strengths and likeable traits. Whilst it is good to know your own frailties, if that is all you know, then you have a very unbalanced view of yourself – one which you would never dream of applying to your very best friend.

When you consider that you can never escape yourself, so long as you live, it is very desirable that you have a balanced and realistic view of who you are. To live with dislike or distaste toward yourself is to condemn you to a lifetime of unrelenting criticism and harsh judgement. If you can be your own worst enemy, you must also have the capacity to be your own best friend. And the further you explore the spiritual world, the more obvious it will become to you that to love yourself is to do yourself the biggest favour you could ever have contemplated.

Make your list of your good and bad points. Be honest. Nobody will ever see this list except you (unless you put it on the fridge under a magnet). You can tell yourself the real truth. And if your bad points seem to outweigh your good points, then consider whether you are not identifying good points within yourself. If the list still does not seem to balance, then consider what you want to alter that would balance things up a little. Remember – when you empower a thing with intent it manifests in the world. What you put your attention on grows bigger.

TWO OF SWORDS

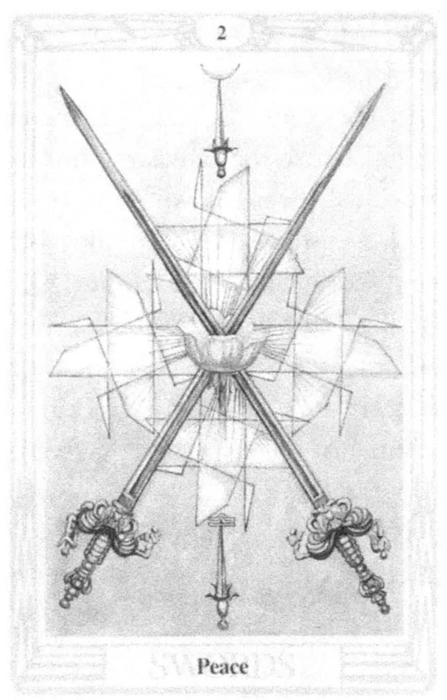

Thoth Tarot - Two of Swords

Two is a number of both polarity and partnership. In numerology, it is seen as the natural attraction which exists between two individuated sources of energy. The 2 of Swords is concerned with the tensions which exist when two opposing elements move into partnership.

The resolution of these tensions is the business of the Lord of Peace. He has the ability to harness that which is useful and positive, whilst discarding anything which stands in the way of amalgamation.

When we engage with spiritual growth, one of the things we strive to achieve is unity between our arcane and mundane Selves. This is no easy task, and forms the cornerstone of growing enlightenment.

It is quite shocking to discover what a wasteland of unexplored territory can lie between our spirits and our everyday personas. Yet the journey into uncharted realms holds great allure once we commit to this pathway.

In our travels we will see the best and the worst in us, often uncovering things which make us feel uncomfortable or disappointed in ourselves. Yet as we begin to become more familiar with the inner terrain, we also discover new strengths, talents and powers of which we had previously been unaware.

By achieving an even-handed acceptance of all that we find within, we will also discover that our darkest acts are often signposts to our greatest potential. Our mistakes can be our greatest teachers. The seeds of our brightness are sown in our shadows.

When we can start this process of acceptance, we empower ourselves to take charge of our lives. We make choices with greater consideration for the consequences. We acknowledge and own our power, treating it with the respect it deserves. And we learn to direct our Will so that it creates the future we dream of, rather than the future we fear.

THREE OF SWORDS

Thoth Tarot - Three of Swords

Everybody experiences pain at some point in their lives... pain is part of the human condition. It warns us of danger or hazard, is a normal consequence of love, and is more regular in its appearance than is most of public transport.

So why on earth do we have such a fearful and uncertain attitude toward it? Many people dread putting themselves in a position where they may be hurt - to an extent that they deny themselves joy, happiness and wonder. They believe that if they were to be hurt they may not survive. Something essential within them would crack and break. They would be unable to recover and live life to the full afterwards.

But they aren't living life to the full anyhow. Fear makes them hesitate on the edge of love and commitment. They estrange themselves from their children, their lovers, their friends, never truly giving everything they have. Imagine a beautiful oasis of pale blue water, rippling softly in a desert wind, perfumed with the heat of the sand. The fearful person is the one standing right at the back under the palm trees, wistfully wishing they were brave enough to throw off their clothes and jump into the water.

When we engage wholeheartedly with life, we open ourselves to the wonder of our world. There are more flowers, more wonderful sunsets, and sunrises, much more in the way of beauty surrounding us. It is true – the flowers might turn into hemlock. But at least we will have seen their beauty before they do that. We will have fed our senses and explored the depths of our beings.

And if, when we do get hurt, instead of running for the nearest corner to hide, we feel, acknowledge and accept our pain, we shall learn something very important. We have the ability to deal with almost anything, because life itself is wonderful, and we are living in its flow, rather than watching from the riverbank. Life has a fascinating way of strengthening and protecting us in our darkest times, even though we may not recognise that. And when we emerge from this present hurt, we will know ourselves to be stronger, more resilient, than before.

Have you ever considered how painful events in your life have contributed to the person you are today? There is a part of our personality which is consistently created by the events we witness. Our responses, our knowledge, our experience, are all constantly shifting and developing. And part of you, the being, changes with it.

FOUR OF SWORDS

Thoth Tarot - Four of Swords

During a period of recovery, as indicated by the 4 of Swords, there are certain essential processes that must take place. Whenever we have encountered trauma, there are important matters to address.

Simply because we have run into trouble, there will be important lessons to be learned. We may have to accept that our lives have changed irrevocably. For example, if we are convalescing from physical trauma, we will probably have made realisations about the way we treat our own bodies, the strength inherent to them, the way we live our lives, and these will need to be incorporated into our future view of ourselves.

The Lord of Truce will come up to mark the restabilisation period after, say, a divorce too. Here, all our expectations about our future have been cast adrift. We are faced, not only with living life without our previous partner, but with many practical considerations as well. We may need to re-assess our working life. We might have suddenly acquired many more responsibilities than before. We may need to move house, or to alter things dramatically within our home environment.

One of the more hidden aspects of the 4 of Swords is that it indicates a kind of withdrawal from the harsh realities of life. When affected this way, we pull back from our everyday responsibilities for a time. This can often be an essential component to begin the healing process. As we gradually recover our well-being and strength we feel more prepared to deal with life's trials.

We tend to give ourselves permission to withdraw when we have been physically unwell. However we are much more unkind to ourselves when the trauma we have passed through is emotional, or event-related. We rarely give ourselves an adequate recovery period when wounded by the less physical type of suffering. Yet we are still as hurt, as stressed, as worn out as we might be in recovering from a heart attack or a broken leg.

We have some unhealthy expectations of our capacity to recover from trying emotional and mental periods in our lives. Almost always we expect to continue working, maintaining certain standards, functioning in a generally 'normal' fashion. We feel ashamed and irritated if we fail to. Indeed, circumstances will often dictate that we have to stick to a normal routine. We cannot get sick leave to convalesce a broken heart.

At times such as these, it is essential that we make a point of making quiet space in which to address our own feelings. All too often we carry on regardless, and as a result fail to heal adequately from earlier pain. We carry our wounds around with us, half-healed or even raw, and they affect what we do as we go through the daily round.

If you are looking at recovering from a wound, whether it be emotional, mental or physical, you need time to feel the pain. Time to examine what this wound means to you. Time to acknowledge and greet every feeling you feel, no matter how contradictory they might appear. It is only by accepting the fullness of your attitude about a given problem, that you begin to understand what you must learn.

It is important to create time in which you can allow yourself to do this if you are on the path of recovery. Of course, you also need to be aware that a person can withdraw from life for too long, and end up finding it difficult to return to its everyday demands.

So, if you are affected by matters covered by the 4 of Swords, remember to book yourself a quality undisturbed hour or so every few days to think about how you're feeling about the difficulties you have passed through. And don't forget to credit yourself wholeheartedly for your progress.

FIVE OF SWORDS

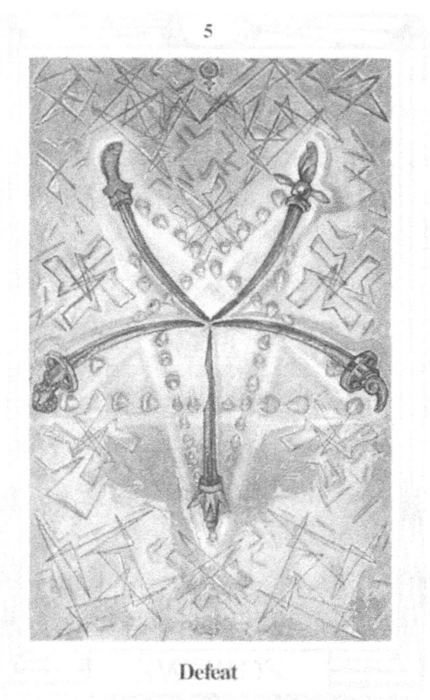

Thoth Tarot - Five of Swords

The Lord of Defeat is not a happy card. It can indicate a range of potential problems when it appears in a reading. All the 5s bring in stress, conflict and difficulty. This is because they relate to Geburah – the Sephirah known also as Power, or Severity. If you consider those two titles for a moment, you might be able to see a little of what the inner lore connected to this card points to. Power, when applied appropriately, can be a very useful life tool. And severe will be the consequence when we fail to handle power with morality and consideration. Again we are looking at how we respond when faced with pain, test or obstacle. This will often dictate the eventual outcome of any given situation. When we approach adversity with courage and grace we stand a great chance of surviving, and obtaining a good result.

Mind you, when something dire has just happened to you, it can be quite difficult to maintain satisfactory levels of courage and grace... especially when we feel much more inclined to go and take our frustration out on the garden wall ;-) It is hard to find your way back into your centre, to feel in tune with yourself and the Universe, when you are shocked, distressed, betrayed. Yet it is at times like these that you most need your still central oasis to be smooth, close at hand, and tranquil.

So we need to find ways of returning to ourselves when pulled to the edges of our lives by events. We need a strategy that we practise so often it becomes second nature, kicking in unconsciously as soon as we feel stormy water on the way. We need a method of protecting ourselves which, whilst effective enough to guard us from our enemies, is not so hard-edged that it shuts out our friends. And we need to be able to trust ourselves.

This method works for me, when I apply it. I look for evidence of what I am to learn from situations around me. It is easier to practise doing this when things are going fairly well, than to suddenly start using the method when our lives have just gone completely haywire.

You can get the hang of the technique by using hindsight to begin with. Look back at a major event which has taken place in your life.

With hindsight you will be able to identify the pattern of unfolding events that created change within you, or altered your life. Imagine the consequences if that event had not occurred. What would be different about you now? What would have stayed the same? Consider the experience you gathered from surviving those events. Do you know something about yourself that you would not otherwise have learned? Did you change direction as a consequence of events – and what would have happened if you had not?

Once you think you have a pretty clear picture (write things down, and keep the notes you made – you will return to them again and again) of the changes a specific event caused, you need to move on to analysing the results. Firstly – are you happy with the outcome? If you are not, chances are you took a wrong turn in there somewhere.

It's worth trying to isolate that point if you can. If you can understand what led to your steps away from your path, you will be less likely to go that way again. If you are basically satisfied, then you did a good job of following your nose.

Once you have gone through this exercise and clarified what you gained and what you lost from a specific situation, turn your attention to examining a conscious decision you made at some point in the past, and subject it to the same rigorous scrutiny.

When you get the hang of doing this (it just takes practice and sometimes outside input) you'll notice that, in among all the suffering, anxiety and uncertainty of these situations, there was a continuous thread of development. And woven into the thread will be the purpose of that particular experience... what you took away from it all.

The next step is to apply this same process to ongoing situations. Think around the problem, decision or whatever from different angles. Ask yourself what you have already learned. Ask yourself where the issues are that remain unfinished. Contemplate what the consequences long-term for you may look like. And whilst you do this, keep returning to your centre. Allow yourself to relax. Acknowledge your emotions, and then give them permission to quiet down long enough for you to think. When you find yourself thinking the same thing twice, stop!! You have gone as far as you are able at this time. So lay the issue down to rest for a while, and get on with your life. Additional pieces of the puzzle will present themselves to you, simply because you have opened yourself to guidance.

SIX OF SWORDS

Thoth Tarot - Six of Swords

For Crowley the 6 of Swords, Lord of Science, represented the heart of the Tarot. That is why the rose cross in the centre of this card is also the design on the back of the whole deck. The rose cross symbol has a long tradition of use in the Hermetic Mystery Tradition, and throughout the Western Mysteries.

It has multiple meanings – most noticeably it is regarded as a symbol of the Great Work in action. The Great Work is regarded as the whole purpose of life and growth into spirit. The completion of the Great Work is conceived as the end goal of all human beings.

The theory is that in the end all living souls will evolve to the point where they can blend harmoniously with pure spirit. Some people take this so far as to say that when the race has sufficiently grown toward purity we will surrender corporeal form and turn into light. On a purely personal level I'm not sure this end result is exactly what I had in mind for perfecting myself. However perhaps there's something I am not yet well enough developed to see here.

The rose cross in this context represents a view of ourselves – the cross is the very heart of us, and we exist first at the outer edges of the card... and of ourselves. Only by making the journey to the cross at the centre shall we fulfil our potential. The card itself shows us how many disparate barriers, thorns, and hidden treasures lay between us and our ultimate goal.

The image on the back of the card is more ordered, but each of the magickal weapons of the four elements is shown – we must gain command both of the weapon and the element in our journey before we can complete our goal. And there are many encounters with these, each bringing fresh knowledge and wisdom, between us and the rose cross at the heart of ourselves.

SEVEN OF SWORDS

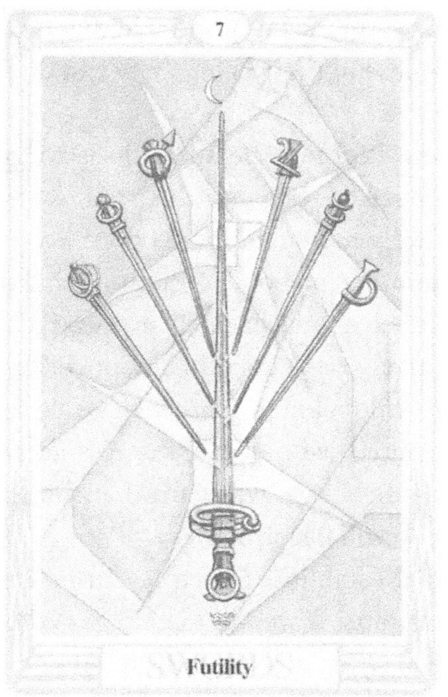

Thoth Tarot - Seven of Swords

We have talked a good deal so far about how in certain circumstances we have to accept that which we cannot change – sometimes conflicts, disagreements and more global issues are outside our scope of influence. Sometimes, no matter how much we do not like something, or an event, we must accept that it exists and get on with the rest of our lives.

However there is a great difference between accepting that certain events have happened then moving on, and resigning ourselves to situations that we regard as beyond our control. To resign oneself tends to suggest inertia. Not only do we accept that a matter exists, but we also often remain in a situation which we find unsatisfactory.

There is an implication here that one surrenders something of value in the process of resigning oneself to a given issue. If that something of value is one's power, then a very dangerous situation will inevitably develop. Some personalities resign themselves easily to inappropriate behaviour, events and circumstances because they believe that, at the core of their being, they can do nothing to change things.

To believe one's efforts to be so futile is to give up a sense of personal impact. Once we fall into this trap, we will find ourselves giving up progressively more and more of our lives – and often we do this in favour of another person. As soon as this decline begins we have created for ourselves an extremely awkward chain of events.

We will find ourselves resigned to accept continually more outrageous actions, and will feel increasingly less able to influence things. The more deeply mired we become, the less access we have to our own power, the less belief we will have that things can change, and the more helpless we will become.

When this spiral establishes itself it can be desperately hard to break free – but we must if we are to gain confidence and a healthy sense of self-respect. Often a person in this situation will have developed the habit of placing other people's feelings, needs and opinions above their own.

When it gets bad enough, the individual may actually no longer be able to reach their own feelings. Layer upon layer of resignation will have built up around the real person within, acting as a buffer of disappointment and unfulfilled dreams.

The way to begin the arduous task of getting out of this mindset is to make contact with the inner self. The mute button needs to be switched to 'off'. People have a right to desire things. We have a right to dream. We have the blessing and terror of imagination – we were intended to use it.

It's a long job working oneself out of the resignation trap. But it is work we owe ourselves if we are to walk in that secret country within, whose landscape is built from the dreams we imagine.

EIGHT OF SWORDS

Thoth Tarot - Eight of Swords

One of the major influences of the Lord of Interference is his remarkable ability to completely negate any skill we have for linear thought. When we are unable to establish a clear and concise line of logic as applied to a given situation or obstacle, we end up going around in circles and eventually disappearing up our own exhaust pipes.

Why particularly would this be an issue when the Lord of Interference is an influence? The clue lies in the title – and also in the design of the Thoth card. Two perpendicular, slightly battered swords border our path... our Will. But these two lay on a bed of all manner of weird shaped blades. Our directed Will is being interfered with – we are being pushed from our path by the ragged spikes on the blades of the underlying thoughts, doubts, fears which lurk in the background of our minds. It is not that we do not know where we want to end up – it is that every effort we make toward our goals is twisted, thwarted, disturbed.

You know the feeling – an event has concerned you. You feel you must do something to alter it. But try as you might, your thoughts do nothing but run around the same old rusty tracks. You reach no conclusions. You make no decisions. You find yourself, again and again, falling into pits of habit in your reasoning.

This process can, of course, be accompanied by those familiar cohorts self-blame and ineffectuality. We can give ourselves a jolly good beating, if we want, during times like these. If we cannot get a handle on a given problem, accept what our spirit is telling us – right now, we do not know how to. There are only two reasons for going over the same ground – one is that we are too afraid to turn the corner into uncharted territory, and the other if that we missed something along the way which is essential to our journey. The latter, whilst frustrating, is often essential – but we do need to go over that old ground with fresh eyes. The former is self-defeating, painful and diminishing to Self.

So – when a given matter gets the better of you, and despite your best efforts, you are making no progress – leave it alone. Don't keep going over it. This simply reinforces the habit that says you must worry everything to pieces, in order to try to resolve it. Perhaps the situation you are concerned with has not, as yet, yielded all the understanding that can come from it. Perhaps something else needs to happen before you can see your way clear to resolution.

Whatever else, do not allow this matter to dominate your life. There will come a point where you know precisely what you need to do, and exactly how you are going to do it. You cannot hurry that moment of clarity. It will arrive when it is time. And in the meantime the rest of your life is happening around you!

NINE OF SWORDS

Cruelty

Thoth Tarot - Nine of Swords

In the Oxford English Reference Dictionary, one who is cruel is defined as being "indifferent to or gratified by another's suffering". I would add heartless and insensitive, possibly affected by sado-masochistic tendencies. This sounds terribly harsh, does it not? None of us would wish to have that word applied to ourselves, and meant unequivocally. We would not want to have to accept that we are capable of cruel acts. And yet, if we are to be true to the greater Truth we all seek – then accept it we must. Not only must we admit to our potential for cruelty, but we must also own and embrace this tendency.

That probably sounds like one of the very least helpful things we could do with a part of our darkness. Why should we consider the depths to which we can sink – what good will it do? Surely it would be more constructive to seek out beauty, joy and love, than to think about the cruelty within? In fact, how many of you are reading this and thinking "But this isn't true of me."?

Oh, yes, it is. The extent of our innate and covert ability to do harm, deliberately, and with no consideration for the consequences, is only outweighed by our amazing ability to deny its existence.

This is precisely how we have got ourselves into this mess we now call life. Our ability to think, scheme, plan, develop, encounter has been fuelled by a constant stream of justification. We have never considered the long term consequences for the direction in which life, and the society we created, were going. And we never considered what effect shirking that responsibility would eventually bring into being.

In refusing to recognise the capacity for sheer cruelty within us, we deny part of our own instinctual nature – a part which is wilful, illogical, and thoughtless. That is why we often only recognise our own cruelties in hindsight. Since we are unwilling to accept that we can be merciless tyrants at times, we cannot objectively assess the effects of our actions or words. Therefore we will not analyse and rectify any mistakes at the time they are made.

This is the truth behind the Lord of Cruelty – the 9 of Swords. Imagine, if you can, a world in which all human interactions were respectful, honest, transparent and loving. A world in which each individual took total responsibility for their actions. A world in which, when there are disputes, each voice is heard and revered for speaking its own truth.

I do not believe that such a world could be created on a half truth... a kind of silent agreement throughout the race that basically most of us are "really good people". We are not. The truth is that all of us have a nasty streak somewhere. And the simple fact is that only by accepting ourselves in our totality, can we begin to find the courage to express into life the deepest truth of what we are.

TEN OF SWORDS

Thoth Tarot - Ten of Swords

Have you ever wondered why the human being tends to learn more from painful, humiliating and fearsome experiences than they do from experiences of pure joy and happiness? Have you ever contemplated why some of the greatest leaps of faith we take, come when we are at our lowest ebb? Have you ever pondered why some of our most significant spiritual breakthroughs occur when all around us lies in tatters?

I would contend that the reason these things happen is because, when everything that we have depended upon, everything we have taken for granted, everything we have seen as constant in our lives is broken, we have nothing left to lose. The reality upon which we have built our days, our consciousness... even our future... has shattered. The things we thought we could rely upon are gone... and instead there is an empty mirror frame before us, mockingly beckoning us forward to who knows where.

When things are going well in life, the last thing we want to do is rock the boat. When the stream of life we travel is relatively untroubled, and the water swift flowing but smooth, we think that everything is fine and dandy. We float through life scarcely touching it. We certainly do not allow ourselves to analyse or question. Why would we want to take the risk?

Yet when something happens to break the safe reflection we have created around us, all of a sudden there are certain harsh truths with which we are faced, whether we like it or not. For instance – all of life is change. Everything alters. If we accept, unmindful, the bounty which surrounds us, we do nothing to ensure that our bounty will continue. We do not consider where it came from, nor consider nourishing it like the growing thing it is. Only when we are faced with a breakdown in our expectations do we begin to question what we contribute.

We have all had the experience of hearing somebody bemoan their 'awful luck', for instance. They talk around the topic, questioning what they have done to deserve such a fate. They say things like "I try to be a good person – why do these bad things keep happening to me?" If they answer their own question honestly enough, the chances are they will eventually find an answer.

But when was the last time you heard a person celebrate their own extreme good luck? When did you last hear a person enter into a fortunate and joyous analysis of how they managed to create a positive stream of energy in their lives? I would guess you have heard the negative analysis far more often than the rejoicing.

The Lord of Ruin is about the way in which we tend to fear danger or pain, and how, when we fear this, we create it. So... rejoice rather than bemoan... celebrate rather than fear. And at all costs, come to understand where the events in your life have their roots.

PRINCESS OF SWORDS

Princess of Swords

Thoth Tarot - Princess of Swords

This Princess has close connections with the ways in which we express our ethics into everyday life. She demands that we live life to the full, face reality and refuse to give in to lower emotions which draw us away from all that we can be when we are at our best. She is a forceful and somewhat intolerant influence, especially when she witnesses unfair and unjust events.

There's another interesting aspect of this Sword court which comes to the fore when injustice and bigotry are ruling. She breaks down old habits which no longer serve their purpose, pulling out accepted routines, submitting them to intense scrutiny. Her ability to cut through rubbish, no matter how established it may seem, is one of her great strengths. She has a way of seeing beyond the surface to the heart of matters, discarding all that is redundant and leaving behind those things which still have inherent value.

Her clarity is essential during periods of spiritual development, because it enables the true seeker to move beyond the external into the realm of truth and growth. She is relentless in her search for truth, and Truths. Her diligence and determination are pretty much unmatched, even among the other Sword Courts.

PRINCE OF SWORDS

Thoth Tarot - Prince of Swords

This observer of life has a lot to teach all of us about how we can use our subtle senses to gain more information in all situations. When this card comes up to represent an actual person you will find that he is the type who tends to sit back and watch what is happening around him. He absorbs atmosphere and nuance, tone and expression, in his efforts to 'read' situations.

We tend to ignore these more hidden methods of communication most of the time. This is a shame, because in failing to thoroughly engage with such information we quite probably perpetuate certain misunderstandings – or even exacerbate them.

The words a person chooses to convey their thoughts reveals a great deal. We tend to unconsciously select words which directly reflect our inner feelings. Even when seeming to be stable and balanced, if we feel – for instance - lonely and depressed, that will show in even the most everyday conversation to an acute listener.

I was waiting in a queue at the bank just before I wrote this commentary. Ahead of me, at one of the tellers' windows, was an elderly gentleman who was paying a power bill. He passed the money and paperwork over to the clerk and said "It's much smaller these days. I should think myself lucky." The woman behind the desk laughed and said "We could all do with that happening couldn't we?" I don't believe she was listening properly. His stance and his tone of voice indicated it was no happy circumstance that lowered his bills – as did the use of the word "should". That implied to me that he felt lucky about nothing at all.

When I am very tired, I not only use appropriate words to describe my tiredness, but also my voice changes. It becomes quite leaden and heavy. I do not smile as often as when I am feeling high on energy, and in tune with life.

Every single person reacts like this to one degree or another. If we train ourselves to engage in the moment, and to keenly observe events as they unfold before us we will learn to understand a great deal more about the people around us.

QUEEN OF SWORDS

Thoth Tarot - Queen of Swords

At the high level of interpretation this Queen corresponds with Athene – goddess of wisdom. This is because the acute insight inherent to the Queen of Swords will, if properly assimilated and integrated, inevitably result in wisdom. Her strengths lie in her ability to separate and identify the distinct patterns which run through a person's life, and to weave these into the fabric of the future.

Wisdom is a hard-won skill... and one which many people do not achieve in the space of one lifetime. Some people believe that if they have extensive knowledge they are, by definition, also wise. But this is simply not true. Wisdom is a great deal more than a collection of facts – or even experience. To be wise means that you not only have these two things – knowledge and experience, but that you also know how to apply them.

I have commented before upon the peculiar human state which leads us to learn more from pain than we do from pleasure. Certainly wisdom can spring more easily from living through and healing from suffering than practically anything else. Perhaps this is because we relate most intensely to our feelings and inner needs when they are gnawing away at us like an incurable tooth-ache. In seeking to relieve the intense pressure this causes, we examine things from a different perspective – in more detail, with greater exactitude – even though we also go around in circles a lot of the time too.

Perhaps this is why, in some traditional commentaries on the Tarot, you will find this card has a very negative interpretation attached to it. In fact, it is sometimes referred to as the Black Widow – along with the Queen of Spades in an ordinary deck of cards. It is true that the card can represent a widow – but there's another connection with Athene here – she is denied the possibility of motherhood, since she must remain a virgin. And one of Athene's totems was the spider.

KNIGHT OF SWORDS

Knight of Swords

I want to examine an aspect of the Knight of Swords more thoroughly that is often avoided – his dark side. In some of the commentaries on

Tarot (especially earlier ones) this card has quite a bad reputation. It can be interpreted to indicate a malevolent man who misuses authority and power.

Certainly in some situations this is a valid definition for the card. When the grace, intelligence and clarity inherent to the Knight become tainted or twisted he can make a dangerous enemy – swift to act, self-indulgent, ruthless in his tendency to go after what he wants without considering anybody else.

There are many similarities between this card and the Magician – each relies on their wits to get ahead in life, both tend to make their own rules and then live by them, each is well-versed in the art of manipulating others. The Magician tends to act with conscious intent, whereas the Knight of Swords tends to be more instinctual in his behaviour.

This card will sometimes come up to indicate a man who is currently unhappy or angry – so the core personality may be better represented by some other court card, and this one will appear to indicate a sudden shift toward negativity.

When a person whose core personality is that of the Knight of Swords has authority over us, we can expect to experience some discomfort if he turns away from the clarity he exhibits when well-dignified. The normal grace with which he exerts his power can become, at worst, tyrannical. There is little point in engaging head-on with this sort of abuse – better by far to remove oneself from the situation as much as possible until the storm has passed.

Regardless of whether you are in contact with a core Knight of Swords, or a man who has shifted into that mode temporarily, it is well worth remembering that manipulation can be a subtle (or not so subtle) perversion of your free Will. Beware falling into the kind of walking trance that has you acting more like a performing seal than yourself. At times when you believe you are contacting the dark side of this Knight it is as well to constantly subject your thoughts and feelings to objective scrutiny in order that you do not lose yourself in his private agendas.

PART V

DISKS

ACE OF DISKS

Thoth Tarot - Ace of Disks

This Ace is elementally cast as Earth of Earth... the very nuts and bolts of material manifest life. This is the earth upon which we stand, the physical actions we take and, more broadly, the entire minutiae of ordinary life.

We often underestimate how completely we are affected by the simple realities of daily existence. It is not unusual, especially in the field of spiritual development, to come across the most outrageously offensive, diminishing and whimsical attitudes toward this most influential area.

People reject reverence of money and status, are derogatory and even envious about those who have more. Some believe that you cannot aspire to, nor achieve, spiritual enlightenment without living in poverty. They say you should not charge for using the fruits of your development – like healing or reading Tarot. They say that to do these things will rob you of your 'talents' – missing the fact that you might have had an innate talent, but that much of what you now know is a hard-earned skill.

All of this is wrong. The Element of Earth is not inferior to any other Element. It is not more preferable to be wealthy in the Element of, say, Air and low on Earthy resources. The ideal state of our relationship with the Elements which combine in our lives is one of balance. We need as much Earth as we do Fire... as much practical security as we have spiritual insight.

Yet again and again, it is the manifestation of the Earth Element in our lives which causes trouble. We grow short of money, threatened by external material circumstances, fearful of our very survival at times.

Our society places an inordinate amount of importance on status and wealth. If we enter into that value judgement, rather than fighting to establish our own, we will find ourselves caught in a desire trap. But in struggling to avoid that fate, we can sometimes go too far the other way, and instead create a poverty trap for ourselves.

We need to allow ourselves the right to have sufficient of everything in our lives. By living a comfortable and secure material life, we free certain energies within ourselves at other levels than the physical. We permit ourselves the liberty of not having to worry about our bills, because we know we can pay them. All that we free energy we free in taking that trusting step can be expended in other ways. The relaxation of spirit we acquire when we are not strangled by scarcity benefits everybody we come into contact with.

So make today the day on which you decide that you have experienced your fill of insufficiency. Make today the day you choose for abundance – in the Earth Element as well as in every other – and allow yourself the right to be open to fulfilment.

TWO OF DISKS

Thoth Tarot - Two of Disks

The Lord of Change always heralds shifting fortunes. Often, there will be major change in a given area of life when this card is dominant, for example, redundancy. This will sometimes be regarded as unwelcome and harmful. But it generally turns out that whatever change has taken place has benefited us to some extent.

Life functions in polarities. We have day and night, life and death, light and dark, positive and negative. Each opposing principle is in constant tension with its counterpart. The skill of creating a rewarding life is that we learn to understand and balance these pressures.

A factor often missed, when examining polarities, is that two apparently contradictory states are, in fact, inevitably interwoven by their paradoxical nature. There is an indestructible link between the principles, say, of light and dark. These concepts reside at the extreme edges of the same thing. We have a complicated set of notions, beliefs and experiences which pivot around our perception of each in our lives. That structure of ideas is part of what we base our reality upon.

Taking command of our life experiences includes developing the skill to balance the seesaw which exists between all polarities. At some point between the seats at either end (opposing principles) is a point of perfect poise. We begin by finding ourselves swept into the air, then down to the depths, again and again. No matter which end of the seesaw we choose to sit on, we shall always find ourselves back on the ground in the end.

When this happens we are caught on the edge of our own awareness. It is difficult to perceive our skills, options and potentials clearly. Our goals are always "up there" above our heads, seemingly unreachable. On those heady, if brief, occasions when we manage to spring upwards, our aims look more possible for a moment. But then down we come again.

When we recognise that our successes and failures, our flaws and strong points, our triumphs and disasters are inextricably linked, we free ourselves to explore the territory which lies between the two extremes. And in so doing, we find that point of natural balance at the centre of our Universe – we become the creature safely balanced at the very top of the Wheel of Fortune – we become the Lord of Dominion (2 of Wands). We rule our own reality.

THREE OF DISKS

Thoth Tarot - Three of Disks

We have discussed the ways in which the human Will can be channelled as a remarkably effective tool, enabling us to achieve our desired result. This card is interesting because it points to using mundane activity and the performance of routine tasks with intent, so that they have an effect upon the rest of life.

Disks are about the material, mundane areas of life – areas which we sometimes tend to get out of balance with the rest of our activities. Either we can become bogged down in mundane matters, and fail to lift our eyes to the skies, or we cannot maintain a healthy and constructive grasp on reality.

Either imbalance is damaging to us. If we do not deal with the details of everyday life, some very nasty things can end up happening to us – the bills don't get paid, the chores don't get done, and the washing basket overflows. Still, we can sometimes regard these tasks in a negative light – we feel that they fail to contribute to our spiritual development, our emotional well-being or our level of knowledge and wisdom. Yet these actions can be regarded as equally constructive as – say - an hour of meditation, or reading an inspiring book.

Rather than just washing the kitchen floor, try doing this whilst thinking about washing away your troubles, or cleansing the world of pain (well, there's nothing like being ambitious ;-). We can convert these seemingly mundane tasks into constructive acts of Will.

If we become bogged down in material matters, this will interfere with our spiritual growth, and limit our horizon. This sometimes happens because the immediate environment is causing worry, or concern – like when financial pressures close their hands around our throats, or when a family member is ill or troubled and this causes pressure.

But it can also happen almost without us noticing – the daily round becomes an almost unconscious cycle. Whilst we are bored, or maybe even dissatisfied, we act like hamsters running around in the same old wheel. The humdrum monotony can only be broken into with decisive action.

If you find yourself caught in this situation, take time out to do something completely different, something which feeds your soul. And look up at the skies!

FOUR OF DISKS

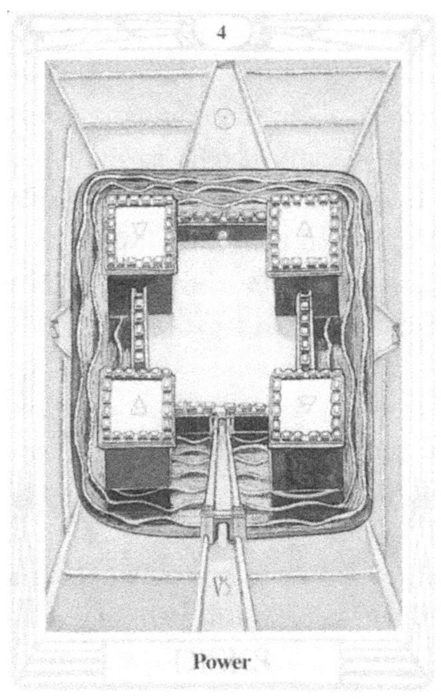

Thoth Tarot - Four of Disks

Early commentators on this card often interpreted it to represent a miser, somebody who hoarded wealth and possessions to the exclusion of all and anybody else. Whilst a simplistic view, it is one which has some basis in truth.

Quabbalistically, all the fours in the deck relate so a Sephirah called Chesed. It is not my intention, just now, to go into an in-depth study of the Quabbala (which would take me a couple of lifetimes ;-) it is sometimes helpful to return to this symbol when studying the Tarot, since the glyph gives us a fresh viewpoint on certain interpretations.

So, very briefly, the concept underpinning Quabbala is that energy, undiluted and formless, is released into the Universe. This energy passes through three Sephiroth before it reaches Chesed. Each of these spheres affects the energy, shaping and channelling it. When it arrives in Chesed, it is converted from pure force into form – and from that point forward is further moulded until it becomes material reality.

The 4 of Disks talks about the mundane aspects of life – house, home, material objects – and it tells us that since all of these are obtained initially from money, they are the result of pure energy... and energy must be allowed to flow or else it stagnates and becomes fetid, poisoning those who are touched by it. So in a sense we can see where the interpretation of this card representing a miser comes from.

However to narrow energy down to a definition purely of money, even in a mundane sense, is to ignore all the other energies which go to make up everyday life – like love, respect and gratitude. We need not be money-rich in order to increase levels of security or attunement with life – we need only to be ready to be grateful for what we have, however little, and to be willing to both give and receive more.

Generosity of spirit has a lot to do with smoothing the wheels which keep daily life rolling, and it comes absolutely free. We sometimes mistake the suit of Disks to only relate to money and material matters, but this is an acute misunderstanding. Disks also relate to basic values in mundane life – our interactions on a minute by minute basis with others. Our behaviour toward others affects them – can shatter their security, challenge their morals, shift their mood. This is part of the wealth we each have as human beings, and we need to be as thoughtful and consciously aware of how we spend that, as we are of how we spend our money.

So, when we examine this card, we need to remember that energy must flow. One way or another we must pass on our bounty, however we interpret that. This is part of what makes life work, and we all have an essential contribution to make. A smile from a stranger can sometimes change somebody's life...

FIVE OF DISKS

Thoth Tarot - Five of Disks

All four 5s in the Tarot bring problems with them, because of their close relationship with the Sephirah of Geburah. I often think of this sphere as the 'forge-fire' of the Quabbala – the place where things are changed by a honing and tempering process.

The method by which a blade is forged has always stood as a useful and descriptive metaphor for human development to me – the heat and flames of the forge represent the trials and tribulations through which we pass in our endeavours, the hammer symbolises the buffeting we can receive along the way, and the cold water is the sudden shock of breakthrough into new consciousness. Life subjects us to much the same process of formation as the finest sword blade.

This card generally covers our mundane environment – the very foundation of our lives. These are the areas, relationships and routines upon which we base our everyday reality. They are areas to which we rarely apply conscious thought, unless we recognise that something has changed. Often the perception of change comes first as a sense of imbalance – things are not the way that they usually are, and consequently we register a break in rhythm that attracts our attention.

Have you ever entered a room in which you spend a great deal of time, and felt a kind of jangling sensation at the back of your mind – then looked around and realised that something has changed? Before you 'jangled' you were paying little conscious attention to your surroundings. You know them so well, you can visualise them without a second thought... until somebody moves a chair without your knowledge, leaves open a drawer you know you had closed. Often, when 'jangled', it takes all of us a moment or two to work out where the discord is. We know something is not right – we just haven't located where.

Most of the familiar areas of our lives are subliminal, like this. Our homes, work places, animals, daily routine, even our relation-ships, are all affected by the 'semi- submerged' factor. Generally this is helpful, assisting us in completing the daily round.

However sometimes the effect can work against us – giving rise to formless and unrecognised worries which eventually take on the scale of full-blown fears. If you find yourself feeling that 'jangle' about a familiar area of your life, do take the time to listen to what you are telling yourself. Acknowledging and owning worries about basic existence frees up a lot of energy for more constructive and happy actions.

SIX OF DISKS

Thoth Tarot - Six of Disks

The Lord of Success is always a welcome card to appear in a reading. It indicates inner harmony, balance and at-oneness with the Universe. Our efforts have paid off – not only do we achieve material success but we develop a sense of self-reliance and self-belief which unshakeable and beneficial. We know, deep down, that we can get what we want out of life, and that we can contribute significantly in any area we choose.

When we have managed to reach this stage in our lives (even if only for a time) there's one particular thing that we need to do. We need to spend time being grateful to ourselves and to the Universe for allowing us such a blessing. Gratitude is a wonderful emotion to express. It allows us to celebrate the good things in our lives, to observe our good fortune and to enter openly into a joyous union with existence itself.

There is a special type of confidence that comes from being grateful. When you consciously acknowledge that you are fortunate, that your hard work has contributed to your happiness and sense of self-content, you begin to recognise that you are a powerful and effective human being.

Knowledge like this is self-perpetuating. Once you see yourself as successful and strong, you begin to realise that, since you achieved this yourself, you can continue to do it. You have the power to create what you need. You have the energy to dream, and to enact your dreams. You can reshape your future into something that more closely resembles your wish for your life.

Nobody can ever take this realisation away from you. It is an inherently personal and unique experience. You cannot learn to feel this way from anybody else – you have to make it within yourself and then acknowledge it. This will see you through difficult times, help you to resolve any problems you encounter, and bring you back again and again, to the understanding that you run your own life.

Of course, if you have not yet fully stepped into this part of you, you need a strategy with which to begin. Start by counting your blessings. All of them. And being genuine in your gratitude. Whilst doing this, recognise that you have created most of this for yourself. You can be grateful for anything – qualities within you, possessions, your career, your relationships... anything at all. There will be good things in your life that you have worked toward. Be proud of yourself for your effort, be appreciative of the circumstances or people that have helped you and, most of all, be grateful you had the opportunity to make those attributes and gather those resources. The more you allow yourself to do this, the more you will have to celebrate.

SEVEN OF DISKS

Thoth Tarot - Seven of Disks

As we have said before, Disks cover the day-to-day matters of family life – or in this case the lack of it, despite the desire. Quabbalistically all 7s relate to Netzach which is a sphere which covers, among other things, Nature, breeding, family and our need for love. These things are particularly important with the 7 of Disks and the 7 of Cups.

We have all gone through periods in our lives where we feel lonely – lacking a partner or mate. Those of us who are lucky have spent more of our time happily inside caring relationships than not. But there are some unfortunate souls who seem to never find fully reciprocal love and tenderness.

This sad state of affairs sometimes has far less to do with bad luck or fate, than it does to do with our deepest feelings about our lovability, and our ability to love. If self-esteem is badly enough damaged, a person can feel unattractive and uninteresting. Whether we mean it to, or not, that lack of self esteem will tend to radiate from us and subtly affect the people we meet.

Of course – it's very easy to SAY that. It is far more difficult to tackle those negative feelings about ourselves and root them out, leaving behind fallow fertile soil in which love can grow.

First and foremost in this battle of emotional weeding is our own ability to recognise the 'lesser' thoughts we have about ourselves. And it is important to acknowledge their power over us. These are pervasive and pernicious little thorns waiting to stab us when we are unwary. But in the battle to meet with our spirit, we must become wily warriors ;-)

Every time you have a deprecatory, insulting or demeaning thought about yourself, write it down. And when you have a little time, sit down and consider what that thought was. Where did it come from? What effect does it have on you if you keep thinking it? Why would you want to think this about yourself?

Once you have managed to answer those questions, you will have the basis for a repair programme in your hands. And then you'll probably be needing to study affirmations ;-)

EIGHT OF DISKS

Thoth Tarot - Eight of Disks

Because this card often heralds a period of rapid mundane or spiritual growth, development and learning, it is necessary to recognise that the demands this places upon us will be great. We need to nurture our own well-being, in order to create the best environment in which to expand. The 8 of Disks demands a subtle energy - balancing process which furthers our progress and expands our potential.

At a deeper level the 8 of Disks teaches us to realistically assess how our personal growth, individual gains and more advanced skills contribute to the whole, which is the society in which we live. In order to move forward in life, we need to be prepared to offer ourselves in service to the whole. Despite the fact that increasingly it seems, people have less sense of community and mutual responsiveness we are, still, one race.

What we, as individuals, choose to contribute toward the overall well-being of our race is our level of service. "Detach from the result" is a phrase that has stuck in my mind ever since it was first said to me. This phrase is very applicable to the concept of service.

If we approach life with an attitude that we need not contribute, we reduce what we receive from life to the same barrenness we offered. But if we give with a happy, full heart then we create bounty and abundance at all levels for ourselves, as well as those we affect. As the 9 of Disks teaches us – what we get is what we give. And we get it with the same decorations as when we sent it out – thorns or bells - the choice is ours.

Service is not hard. It can be woven into our daily routines until we do not even think about performing acts of service. The smallest thing can make a difference if it done with a heart full of light. Hold the door open for the women with the pram and packages next time. Get the groceries down off the high shelf for a shortie like me. Give a person chance to cross the road in safety, even if it does delay us for a minute.

If we take a look at what we spend most of our time doing – like work - there will be opportunities of service there. People can sometimes make the mistake of thinking that because they do not do a 'meaningful' job, they cannot turn their occupations into opportunities for service – but this is not true in almost all cases. We can treat the people with whom we deal with respect and politeness. We can choose to be as helpful as we are able. These ideas can be woven into almost any job.

Remember that when you decide to better yourself in some way, you are not only making an investment in your own future, you are also working to be of greater service to the community. Purely by studying and learning in order to achieve a skill, or an insight, you make a contribution to the race – your attempts to enlighten yourself add to the flame that is the human spirit.

NINE OF DISKS

Thoth Tarot - Nine of Disks

The hidden lore of the Lord of Gain, 9 of Disks, concerns the movement of energy. What we put out is, fundamentally, what we get back. It relies entirely on the concept of the Laws of Attraction – we attract forces and events to us with our every thought, word and action.

We can see watered down versions of this belief in concepts like positive thinking... however to an extent such pop psychology ideas miss the point of the process entirely. We do not alter our circumstances purely by consciously thinking positive thoughts and refusing to harbour any negative ones – and anyhow, very few of us are able to achieve this long term. It is our actual mindset which needs to shift if we are to employ the Laws of Attraction.

We not only need to lift the level at which we think consciously – we need to shift the very roots of our conceptions and consciousness. Even our incessant monkey-mind chattering has to work in accordance with the Law. We have to believe ourselves worthy to receive bounty and affluence before it will flow, with ease, into our lives. We have to let go of survival fears and safety nets, and simply hurl ourselves into the process of rightful living.

We also need to examine our innermost beliefs about concepts like whether there is sufficient in the world to go round. Only by abandoning our belief in lack, can we direct ourselves toward a bright and happy future, filled with abundance and satisfaction.

The question of service is crucially important here. If we are unwilling to give of our abilities and talents freely, as well as have a healthy understanding of what they are actually worth, then we give only in small portions to life. Life will give in small portions back. If we resent what we give, rather than giving with an open heart, then we give to life churlishly. Life can do churlish too ;-)

So, underpinning the Laws of Attraction and the way they function, is the requirement for a great deal of personal responsibility and honesty. We have to know where are our Achilles' heels, our negative reactions, our tendencies to do less than our best. And we have to accept these without judgement, so that we free ourselves to work openly on them in order to shift perspective.

And finally, we need to remain aware, as much as possible, of our motives for doing what we do. We need to be alert to the times when we stray off the path, and we need to be ready to bring ourselves to book for anything we do which does not contribute positively to our own lives, and to life itself.

TEN OF DISKS

Thoth Tarot - Ten of Disks

We have talked about not hoarding – money, energy, positive thought patterns. This is the inner meaning of the 10 of Disks, Lord of Gain. It points to a simple, yet oft- overlooked, fact about life.

It is in constant motion. Nothing remains the same for more than a second. The planet we live on constantly revolves and circles. The solar system our planet belongs to never ceases to trace its eternal course. Our own bodies are hives of activity, even when we believe ourselves to be still. And if anything in that mighty dance tries to remain the same, it will either be battered to pieces by the force of the movement of all else, or it will become fetid and stagnant

There are some very tight links between the Lord of Gain and the Lord of Change (2 of Disks). The 2 warns that if we are unable to accept the changing manner of life, we shall bring ourselves to a Tower moment with such ruthless inevitability that we will regret our tardiness earlier. And the 10 shows us what happens when we allow life to flow through us in a constant, ever-shifting stream.

The thing that generally causes the problem when we are faced with change is fear. We fear that we lack the ability to adapt – yet this is a fallacy since we are adapting at all times. Many of our body's physiological functions are geared to automatically adapt as conditions change – if it's cold our bodies conserve warmth, if we run our hearts beat faster to re-oxygenate. How on earth have we developed this belief that our minds are any less capable of adapting?

When we can accept change with equanimity, we empower ourselves to attune more closely with life's forces. Even change we do not invite will bring new horizons if we allow it to. And if we surrender our fear of change, we are more readily able to initiate necessary changes with the least possible disturbance.

PRINCESS OF DISKS

Thoth Tarot - Princess of Disks

In my earlier analysis of this card I talked briefly about the inherent strength of a person represented by the Princess of Disks and also touched upon the concept of the rosa mundi. In the years that have passed since I have often been asked to expand upon both of these topics. Find that commentary here.

In fact, they are inter-related. The rosa mundi originally arose from alchemical belief, but has since been widely employed in a variety of areas (there is an actual rose named this now). The Rose of the World is red, and represents the blood of the Goddess, Empress or Queen. In alchemic lore the King and Queen are repeatedly sacrificed and re-created in order to bring abundance and growth.

Just as the sword's blade is continually heated, forged and cooled in the process of tempering, so are we humans. For those of us who have chosen to make this a conscious path through which we grow and expand, both in knowledge and understanding, life's experience is probably our greatest teacher. Just as the blade is scorched by fire, we are scalded by pain; just as the blade is hammered, so are we battered by events; just as the blade is plunged in cold water, so are we dashed in the face by shock and surprise. And hopefully, from these experiences, we learn.

What we learn is that we are stronger and wiser than we were before. And we will have understood something more about our own reserves of inner strength. As a result, we make conscious contributions to the shaping of our own future.

I think one of the reasons that we tend to learn more as a result of suffering pain is because when we are hurt we focus on the feeling intensely – time stops. The past and the future have less relevance than they do when things are going well. All that counts is the feeling. When we are this focussed, we actively engage with life – omens, portents and coincidences assume greater importance, we hear the whisper of our intuition more clearly, we use our senses more thoroughly. When we do this, we open the door to spiritual leaps of growth.

However the Princess of Disks provides a quicker and less painful way of acquiring that understanding. Her quiet, abiding strength comes from her ability to put her attention in the moment. When we are able, for a second, to still the clatter of yesterday and tomorrow, we also become able to attune our senses and focus our attention. We become more aware of information coming from the subtle senses. And at times like these we may attain revelation and fresh understanding without the necessity for pain or fear to focus us.

The secret here is the art of 'right attention' – allowing your Self to live your life to a greater degree. This is an incredibly difficult skill to learn, but it's well worth working on getting the knack. The more you allow yourself to live in the moment the more your spirit will make itself heard. Remember – you are a being of light. At the highest reaches of your being, you really do have all the answers to your own questions... you do know how to shape your life. The only thing you need to do is remember how – and that begins by reaching towards the very heart of you.

Make a point of simply stopping. Whatever you are doing, just stop. And for a few seconds allow yourself to absorb what your senses tell you. Pay attention to what surrounds you, and listen to the thoughts your mind is thinking. Every time it wanders off topic, bring it back to the moment. If you practise often enough, you will gradually achieve the art of 'right attention'.

PRINCE OF DISKS

Prince of Disks

Thoth Tarot - Prince of Disks

One of the important aspects of the Prince of Disks is his way of teaching us to work unfailingly toward a goal. We can dream as much as we like – we can create the most phenomenal fantasies about what our lives could look. But if we are not prepared to formulate those dreams into a series of goals, each marking a stage in our journey toward our desires, they will never ever come true.

When people set themselves a momentous goal, they then have to break the achievement of that goal into manageable sized chunks. When we look up at the top of the mountain from the foothills, we recognise that we have a very long way to go if we are ever to reach the summit. The task ahead can be overwhelming… where to start? But if we turn our eyes from the skies to the ground in front of us the process of beginning becomes clearer. We simply have to walk the first few yards, and we will have begun our climb.

When we decide that we want to create something in our lives, we choose to climb a mountain. We need to have very clear in our minds the end desired result. Then we need to work out how to achieve that.

For instance somebody is living in rented accommodation and has only been employed for six months. Their desire is to buy a property of their own. First and foremost they must raise a deposit. This will entail working hard and spending little, so that they can save. That process serves a double purpose because the time spent saving will count toward their viability as a borrower when they apply for finance. If they work with the constant intent to buy a home of their own, every working task is converted into an expression of Will toward the desired result, as is every deposit into their savings account. Each day becomes a concentrated energy stream toward their new home. They are pouring their energies into achieving what they need, just as does the Prince of Disks.

Life responds freely to our intent. If we are clear in our objective, determined that each act we take shall become an act of directed Will, and we do the physical and practical things that carry us toward our desired result, it will appear.

If we find ourselves thwarted, or pulled from our chosen objective often, then we need to examine ourselves carefully to find out what is going wrong. Have we chosen the wrong aim? Do we doubt that we can make it happen more often than we believe we can? Is it right for us? All these factors will enter the equation. But in the end, if we are prepared to direct ourselves toward something with clarity, honesty and sheer determination, life will release to us that which we have already built to perfection in our minds.

QUEEN OF DISKS

Thoth Tarot - Queen of Disks

Each of the Queens has the inner title of Queen of the Throne of (insert elemental attribution here) so this card is also known as the Queen of the Throne of Earth. This title refers to the deep meaning behind the card – that of growth and fertility. Most representations of this card show lush vegetation, and often animals.

She rules over all aspects of procreation, with special reference to sex and sensuality. In fact all the Disk Courts have an underlying connection with sex, from the deep and half hidden passion of the Knight and Prince through to the enduring strength and power inherent to the two female Courts.

This society of ours has dealt us something of a raw deal when it comes to the whole area of intimate physical activities. We have a whole array of faulty belief, inhibitions, hang-ups and misconceptions to choose from when attempting to develop our relationship to our sexual selves – and precious few good examples to learn from.

Rather than seeing sex as a perfectly natural and instinctual activity, it seems that we alternately place too much and too little importance on it. We vacillate madly between worshipping and abhorring it. And when we examine the way that we have degraded the act we discover some of the most repulsive behaviours of our race.

The Queen of Disks teaches us to return to the question of sex with an open mind. We need to be aware of those areas in which we have absorbed some of the negative energy surrounding the act... that way we can begin to untangle our feelings and come to a better understanding. If we can create a healthy attitude toward our own sexual desires, changes will begin to take place at all levels of our being.

It's important to root out the 'mucky' bits that we have allowed to grow up inside. This leaves us free to attune comfortably with our instinctual needs. Everybody collects 'mucky' bits about sex one way or another. But we need to give ourselves permission to evolve in this area as much as in any other.

If you know you have inhibitions do not hide from them. Get them out of the cupboard and examine them. Ask yourself all the questions we have posed before... why do you think this? Which experiences contributed to you holding this view? What does it cost you? What benefits does it bring? How would you feel if you had a different point of view?

When you've finished you will discover that you have, at the very least, brushed the dust off your inhibition and acknowledged it as your own. At best, you will decide not to think that any more ;-)

KNIGHT OF DISKS

Thoth Tarot - Knight of Disks

This card contains the secrets of one particular path of growth and development – in fact, each of the Knights relates to a different method of following our guiding star. Whilst one may be our favourite and most regularly used method, we will use all of them at different times, and in different circumstances.

The Knight of Disks leads us to study the natural cycles that surround us constantly. When we observe the passage of time, the growth of plants, the alternating seasons, the changing moons, we see an inevitable and undeniable spiral of growth. This infinitely detailed and mostly predictable pattern emerges as a continuous expansion which proceeds unaffected by anything else.

Everybody has periods in their spiritual journey where they feel they are marking time. These can be painful and lonely experiences. We have no true sense of whatever we regard as our gods. We feel estranged from the explosions of spiritual revelation that fill us with wonder. We are bereft of trust and acceptance. And we fail to see that, whether we know it or not, we are still growing. The barren periods in life are often preparations for new development.

What we often lose sight of in times like these is that we are still changing inside. We are the seed lying dormant below the surface of the soil, waiting for the sun's warmth to coax us into awakening. A seed waiting for the sun does not believe it is doing nothing, making no progress. It recognises that there is a lot of difference between lying fallow and being barren.

This is the message that the Knight of Disks brings to us - That when we feel empty, directionless, confused we need to focus our attention on the cycles of life. We need to watch the way that things change around us and recognise that we too are changing – even though we just don't yet know how. We need to allow ourselves the time to lie fallow, to feel feelings which seem to be holding us in one spot, to acknowledge our fears, our doubts, our hurt and pain.

We need to accept that emotions we might see as frustrating, saddening, painful are a natural part of being alive. They are part of our experience. By truly feeling our feelings we allow ourselves to pass through them and gain perspective and renewal.

So... when you are in a Knight of Disks phase, sit and watch the seeds germinate. As they grow, your new direction will emerge.

PART VI

EXERCISES

THE AURA EXERCISE

First, seat yourself comfortably and then establish a regular breathing pattern. Take long slow even breaths and exhale gently. Shortly you will find yourself becoming aware of areas of tension within your body. Systematically release these knots of stress and allow yourself to become progressively more relaxed. Pay attention to passing thoughts which skim across the surface of your mind. Gradually clear everyday pressing worries away.

When you have dealt with your immediate thoughts begin to imagine that there is a sphere of brilliant white light above your head. This sphere spins slowly, and as it does the light which emanates from it flashes and sparkles. Sometimes you feel as though you can see within the sphere. The light grows steadily brighter until it glows upon your head, hair and your face. The glow becomes more and more intense until it gleams upon your shoulders, enveloping your head in radiant light.

Now this light spreads down your body and across your legs until around you there is a most perfect luminous glow. The sphere above your head becomes still brighter and brighter until its brilliance obscures the outside edge and, instead, it looks as though there is a shining star above your head.

The glow which surrounds you is rich warm blue and it swirls with the turning of the sphere. Here and there iridescent mother of pearl shimmers and gleams. Sometimes flashes of brilliant green light spot in your aura.

And still the sphere above your head becomes brighter and brighter, until suddenly rays of intense blue white light spill out from the sphere down your body. You are enveloped in a shimmering cloud of light. It spreads out beyond you for several inches and within it there are radiant silver sparkles - brilliant particles of light which touch your skin in whispers, causing little ripples of energy wherever they rest on you.

Notice how your aura seems to move clockwise around your body, scintillatingly bright, shining and beautiful. Make this image as real as you possibly can. Feel the warmth of the glow which surrounds you. Breathe in the power and the energy of the light. Feel your skin tingle where the sparks of light touch it.

And most of all, know that this is yours. Now, draw in the edges of your aura. Draw them in toward your body and see the colour there intensify and become a deeper stronger shade of blue. See yourself surrounded by shimmering blue white light which is edged by azure. Experience the power and force which flows through your body.

When you decide that you have exercised for long enough allow yourself to become aware of your surroundings. Hear the noises of the World. Smell its scents. When you open your eyes remember that your aura is still there. It envelops you, indisputably real and perfect.

You are surrounded by light.

THE LESSER BANISHING RITUAL

This exercise cleanses the space over which you perform it, and banishes negative influences from your sphere. It can also be used as a protective device in any situation where you feel threatened. You will find it a useful process to carry out when you feel uneasy in your surroundings, when you feel that the atmosphere has been polluted, or when you are feeling vulnerable and unhappy.

At first, the exercise must be worked physically, because this is the best method of learning the process, and creates the strongest form of the exercise in terms of results. The size of Circle inscribed (and therefore the space cleansed and protected) may be contracted or enlarged with practice. You can create a tiny Circle around yourself to strengthen and harden the aura, or alternatively cast a wide Circle to enclose a house, say. However, be aware that the further you attempt to throw the Circle the greater will be the power required to erect and maintain it.

The exercise consists of four parts:

- ONE Quabbalistic Cross
- TWO Inscription of the Pentagrams

- THREE Invocation of the Archangel
- FOUR Quabbalistic Cross

So now we'll look at how to do each part and then put it all together at the end.

ONE - How to perform the Quabbalistic Cross

You work the Cross before and after the rest of the process in order to ensure your own balance.

Firstly, extend the first two fingers on the right hand.

Touch your forehead, and say:

"Ateh" (A-tay)

Touch your groin, and say:

"Malkuth" (Mal- koot)

Touch your right shoulder and say:

"Ve geburah" (Vay geb-oo-rah)

Touch your left shoulder and say:

"Ve gedulah" (Vay ged-you-lah)

Touch your heart and say:

"Leolam" (Lay-oh-lahm)

Cross your arms on your chest with hands to shoulders (right arm over left) and say:

"Amen".

You have drawn a cross over your body, and said "You are (yourself) the Kingdom, the Power and the Glory, forever and ever, Amen". You may note the familiarity of these words!

Having conquered the movements and words, you must now build up a visualisation to go with the actions. Without the visualisation, the Cross has less power and effectiveness. When you touch your forehead, imagine that there is a sphere of light above your head. When you draw your hand down to the groin, you also draw down the golden light from the sphere. Visualise this as a ray of light which spreads all the way down through your legs, and penetrates the ground beneath your feet. When you draw your hand from shoulder to shoulder, as you cross the midpoint where the ray of light penetrates you, imagine that it floods out sideways in both directions.

Your body is now centred on a glowing golden cross. Hold this image for a few seconds until you can feel the energy of the visualisation permeating your physical body.

TWO - Inscription of the Pentagrams

The inscription of the pentagrams is performed at each quarter of the Circle, and a Godname is sounded in each pentagram to empower it.

A pentagram is a five-pointed star. Each of the points belongs to a given Element. You require the Earth Banishing Pentagram (this banishes in the Element of Earth, and therefore removes mundane and material influences from your sphere). It is inscribed in the following fashion:

Using the first two fingers of your right hand as in the Quabbalistic Cross, extend the arm and, beginning in line with the left hip, draw a line which ends in front of your forehead. Then extend the line down to your right hip. Now continue to inscribe across to opposite your left shoulder. Move your arm horizontally to opposite the right shoulder and then back down to your original starting point before the left hip. Then pierce the pentagram in its centre and sound the appropriate Godname.

THREE - Invocation of the Archangel

The invocation of the Archangels is performed in the centre of the cleansed area because in performing the inscription of pentagrams you have created a kind of vacuum, a place in which no influence exists. Therefore you need to fill it with something beneficial.

OK, FOUR is the same as ONE so let's put it all together.

THE LESSER BANISHING RITUAL

Facing East, work the Quabbalistic Cross. Then stand in the centre of the working area and extend the right hand, first two fingers outstretched and turn slowly around, drawing a Circle in the air. Envisage this as either a stream of glowing blue-white light or as flames, flowing from the fingertips.

Again, facing East, inscribe the first Earth Banishing pentagram in the air, visualising it in light or fire.

Pierce the middle and vibrate the Godname:

JHVH (Ya-HOE-wah) or (Yah-WAY)

Keeping the arm outstretched, turn to face the Southern Quarter, and inscribe the next pentagram.

ADNI (ADD-on-eye)

Turn to face the Western Quarter, and inscribe the pentagram.

EHIH (Eh-HEE-yay)

Turn to face the Northern quarter and inscribe the pentagram.

AGLA (Ag-LAA)

Turn again to face the East, and stand with arms outstretched, palms upwards. Maintain the visualisation of the Circle and the pentagrams in your mind.

Say the following: "Before me, Raphael, Behind me, Gabriel, On my right hand, Michael, And on my left hand, Auriel, About me flames the pentagram. And above my head shines the six-rayed star."

Then complete the Quabbalistic Cross.

The Lesser Banishing Ritual should be completed every morning and evening after sunrise and sunset, and thereafter at any other time when you feel you need to either strengthen your defences or to cleanse the inner area. You will become more and more proficient at its performance with practice.

Once you are proficient at constructing personal LBRs you may extend the area you cover with it, by visualising the stream of light flowing further out away from your body. In this way you can cover relatively large areas.

You may also construct LBR's around things like cars, before starting a journey. Sit inside and raise the defence, then off you go!

A NOTE FROM ANGEL PATHS

First of all, we'd like to thank you for buying this book. Together with the people who support Angel Paths, you are keeping alive the idea that Jan devoted much of her life to.

We (Ellie and Graham) first met Jan in the late eighties when she was running face to face Tarot courses. Those courses went on to become the backbone for both this book and the website. And Jan went on from our Tarot teacher to become our friend. So, when she passed away in June 2019, she was already talking about passing the business to us when she retired. We respected her wish that the website and teaching lived on.

We've done what we can to honour her legacy and enable her words to reach as many people as possible.

With that in mind, we've done our best to tidy up the books, bring them into line with what readers would expect, while at the same time preserving the voice of Jan. Anyone who met her, either in real life or online, will know that she had a wicked sense of humour and a unique way with words and we hope this shines through in this book.

We've also kept the Card of the Day going. Every business day (in the UK) we pick a card, send it out via email, and post it on the Angel Paths Page on Facebook. It's a great learning experience to focus on one card at a time. If you wish to be added to the list, please go to the Angel Paths website and you can sign up from there.

As always, you're more than welcome to get in touch with corrections, comments, memories or anything else at admin@angel-paths.com.